This book is dedicated to Silvia Viviani and all the other amazing volunteers at Torre Argentina Cat Sanctuary in Rome

To thank them for their endless hard work and care of the cats who have all become so dear to me

To the memory of Lia who along with Silvia never gave up on her dreams and made this cherished place a reality

They remind me to always have courage, follow my dream and to enjoy every day in life

Thank you!

GW00400246

Torre Argentina, a special little place. One which overwhelms the senses and brightens the heart. I can write and talk all day long about this special place but really you must go there to feel it, to see it and sense it. I can only describe it by saying that when you do visit once you will certainly leave a little piece of you heart there and when you return home a little piece of the shelter returns with you.

The Area Sacred is very famously known for being the place where Julius Caesar was assassinated. A large square filled with ruins of temples but when many people stand and admire the history which lies before them they are often surprised to see something moving. They look and find it is a cat and before their eyes they will spot many more cats moving freely among the ruins. These cats are the free cats, the cats which are too feral to stay inside and who make their own choice to remain there together. Some of these cats will find a partner and remain together for life, so although it may seem a very solitary life it can often be the best life for they are free, they have food and care and they find companions of their own kind.

In 1993 two ladies together started to help take care of the stray cats of Rome. Lia Dequel and Silvia Viviani were quick to realise that with the cat population growing at a super-fast rate they needed to do more and so in 1994 Torre Argentina was created. The birth of the shelter allowed many more cats to be fed but most importantly the start of the ongoing campaign to trap neuter and return many of the feral cats. The only way to keep the population down is through sterilisation.

At that time many people were either ignorant to the ways in which the cats would breed unnecessarily or they simply just did not care. Many of the cats found at the shelter were either abandoned by their owners when it was vacation season, or they became bored with their new pet and simply did not want it. The sterilisation programme continues today with most years offering around 4000 sterilisations to the cats of Rome and if times are more prosperous then that number only increases.

The shelter, home to around 130 cats offers adoptions of healthy cats, rehomes kittens and provides end of life care for the sick and injured cats, the ones who would suffer unimaginably on the streets if they were left alone, ultimately to die. This work is significant, yet as always, everything in life is a cycle. Through the presence of the nursery cats and office cats the distance adoptions raise money which allow the imperative sterilisation works to continue. Through this work even more lives are spared. Less cats will enter the shelter in terrible conditions because the cat population will eventually decrease. It is near impossible to never have a single stray or feral cat on the street and cats have always played a big part in the culture and history of Rome, but the shelter strives to save, to help, to heal and repair and prevent further suffering where possible.

The cats who enter and who are on the distance adoption programme really are in some ways a gift. A gift to us because we can enjoy them, know them, understand them and love them. However, they are also a gift in the way that they allow the necessary funds to be received and this money is vital for Torre Argentina to carry out its important work.

Through distance adopting one cat you are saving the life of another.

Lia sadly passed away on July 3rd, 2013 and yet despite her passing it is strongly felt by many of the volunteers that her presence is still around, and she comes to them when they need her most. For Silvia Viviani this loss must have been the greatest sorrow but still she continues to carry out her important work and finds strength in feeling her friend is beside her, always.

Today the Torre Argentina grows in strength and indeed numbers, with supporters across the world ready to embark on a "Global Gathering". The first of its kind to be hosted at the wonderful venue of Hotel Forum in the centre of Rome with many of its strongest supporters making their way from all over the world. Coming from places as far as Australia, America, Europe and UK the support is heavy in numbers and strong in heart.

This introduction only goes some way to explaining the beginnings of life at Torre Argentina, for me the best way to learn is to come, to spend some time here, to speak to the volunteers, to speak with Silvia Viviani if you are lucky enough to call when she is around.

To understand the work that they do is to see it.

Visit, listen, watch and learn, make sure to visit the nursery too for that is a truly special place, sad, yes, but also heart-warming. You will be amazed and overwhelmed at this special place. However, please remember to donate on the way out or purchase a gift. No donation is too big or too small and all are gratefully received. All the monies contribute to the ongoing sterilisation programme which is principal in sparing the lives of many more cats from unnecessary suffering from living alone on the streets.

All profits from sales of this book will be given directly to the Torre Argentina to help them continue their work, in the memory of Lia, to honour Silvia Viviani, a true hero, to honour all the wonderful volunteers who mean so much to me, Monica, Silvia, Valentina & Daniele to name only a few and in memory of my own little Gianburrasca who you will read about in this book.

Thank you for supporting the Torre Argentina, a place so very dear to my heart and for me a place that defines everything that is great, wonderful and magical in the world.

Gianburrasca

I mentioned earlier about a cat named Gianburrasca and in some ways he is the passion which drove me to write this book.

I started to follow the work of Torre Argentina after a visit to Rome and since then have built up wonderful friendships from all around the world.

I was so lucky to have met Gianburrasca for he became quite a famous cat known to many around the world.

When I heard from Silvia that Gianburrasca had passed away my heart broke into a million pieces.

Just the same morning I had happily uploaded a video I had made for him to celebrate him and everyone's memories of him.

A compilation of beautiful photos showing how much he was loved and is loved all around the world and the anticipation of all those who were coming soon to meet him could be felt from the images on the screen.

How is it possible that such a tiny being can have such an impact on everyone?

Well this is Gianburrasca and he had the heart the size of the universe. His love was endless just as my love for him and so many others who feel the same.

A tiny boy who captured us the second we saw him, met him or held him. I didn't think it was possible to love another after losing my own two cats but Gianburrasca found a way into my heart.

All he wanted was to be loved and to love and this was what he gave in endless supplies and indeed he received.

This is how I will remember him.

My beautiful boy from Rome.

So, because of Gianburrasca I have spent many hours writing for the Torre Argentina, I have never enjoyed anything as much as the work I do for them.

After all anything to do with cats is enjoyable and its easy too!

Last year I trained for nine months to complete an ultra-marathon of 35 miles on cross country terrain, a difficult race and I dedicated this race to Gianburrasca to keep his memory alive.

The support over the whole nine months was overwhelming. I could not have ever imagined in my wildest dreams how people would get on board and support such a thing. Yet it happened.

Relentless and with much passion the supporters often seemed to have more energy than I did and for me this meant everything.

Every step was worth so much to help the cats I had grown to know and love over time. Thank you to each one of you who supported me.

This book was written as a celebration of the Torre Argentina, to help them from the money raised from any purchases of it and to celebrate the cats.

To give each cat a voice, to share their stories which I enjoy writing but to reach, hopefully, a wider audience. The more people who know and understand our cats the more people there are to love them, to adore them just as we do. The more support there is for Torre Argentina the more cats who can be saved.

The cats really have become everything to me, the volunteers on the ground in Rome do such amazing important work and for me they are also everything. In my eyes they are true heroes.

Working tirelessly every single day to provide great care and attention to every single cat when they need it most is the most beautiful gift they can ever give to an animal and those who come to Torre Argentina in my eyes have reached their very own paradise.

For many of those cats the conditions they arrive in would make you sit in the corner and just weep however these volunteers are strong. They cannot sit and weep, they must spring into action and do what they know best. Fix, heal, repair, restore and mend.

All of this is done with love, kindness and passion. I always say if you have love and kindness then you have everything, but the passion is the fire in their bellies and is what pushes them to continue even when they face difficult days.

When they must do the unthinkable and accompany our beloved ones over the rainbow bridge when that time comes.

They do what we cannot because we are not there every day, we don't always see this side of the story, but we must know it to fully understand just how hard it is and how special these volunteers are.

I write the tributes for the cats who pass away and each time a piece of my heart floats off up to that rainbow bridge to join the cat I am writing about but then another cat arrives and brings enough love with them to fill that little hole which was empty and broken, and it repairs, just the same as the lucky cats who end up in our shelter.

One of the most important tasks carried out by the Torre Argentina but which is not talked about enough is the amazing work they do in their sterilisation programme. Year on year the numbers of sterilisations carried out grows. Of course, it is only as successful as the funds allow them to be, but this work is vital.

Yes, it is important to save the lives of those who come into the shelter in critical condition and to help them, but the sterilisations prevent more kittens being born, prevents them being injured, blinded, killed by cars. It spares them facing a life on the streets and ending up like those who come to spend their last days with us.

This sterilisation programme saves lives. It is important, and when you come to the shelter just because you don't "see" it since it is not visible just remember that it is significant. If could even be the most vital thing that they do.

This book is written starting with a little poem I wrote one afternoon. It's just fun and something light but which sums up the Torre Argentina if it is possible in just one poem.

Following the poem are the stories of many of the cats who are or were on the distance adoption programme. Most were written for our Facebook group, but have been extended and updated for the original stories are older and much time has passed for many of these cats, we know more about them and we have funny anecdotes to write about too.

Finally, I finish the book with the tributes to just some of the cats who have passed over in the past twelve to eighteen months. Each one was named, each one honoured and most of all each one loved and none of them will be forgotten.

This book is my way to say a small thank you to everyone at Torre for the unconditional love and care you have given to the cats and my sweet Gianburrasca over the years.

I cannot thank you for enough what you have done during his life.

Thank you to Silvia for being there to help him over the rainbow bridge. Thank you, Monica, for the videos you sent me and for always updating me on how he was doing.

Every cat is special but for me Gianburrasca was the one. I hope everyone will keep his memory alive. I know I will, and I will never forget him.

I love you Gianburrasca and thank you for what you brought to my life. Sleep well and look after all the other angel babies because we know it's what you do best.

Supporting Torre Argentina

Please support the Torre Argentina by visiting their website where you can read our news and find out more about the cats.

 You can also send money through PayPal or choose a cat to adopt at a distance.

The distance adoption scheme is a gesture or symbol if you like, to say the cat is supported by your donations, however funds go towards care for all the cats and of course the sterilisation scheme.

https://www.gattidiroma.net/

Write to us or visit us at
Colonia Felina Di Torre Argentina
Associazione Culturale
Largo Di Torre Argentina
Dentro Gli Scavi (Archeological)
Angolo Via Florida E Via Arenula
00186 Rome

Email us
torreargentina@tiscali.it

Join our Facebook group for news, stories, videos and to make new friends, become a part of the TA family, everyone is welcome

Gatti Di Roma – Roman Cats

A little gesture can go a long way!

A little Poem - Torre Argentina

Torre Argentina
A place we all should know
In the centre of the ruins
A place where love does grow

A large square filled with history
And old temples galore
But most importantly
It's the place where tigers roar

Known for Julius Caesar
Where he fell unto his death
In this place he found his end
And took his dying breath

But today this place is different
It's more special you may see
For here it is now cat heaven
such a wonderful place to be

My words can't quite describe it
You must visit there yourself
For when you come you will never leave
Put your heart upon the shelf

This huge city filled with history
And stories all around
But this one here at Torre Argentina
Is the most special to be found

A place to help the wounded
The sick ones and the blind
A home, for life, forever
When they come here they shall find

Not one more special than another
All equal and the same

All loved with heartfelt measures
Each one given a name

We love these cats so dearly
They are so special indeed
These cats who come to us
Are all desperately in need

We have some for a long time
And others not so much
But each one who passes through our door
Is given so much love

They find a life that's different
From the one they knew before
To some a new experience
to heal where once was sore

Warm beds and blankets
Cat trees and treats
Chicken parties on Sundays
And yoghurt through the week

Always people to visit
And give them lots of love
Cats surely sent from heaven
Gifts from up above

All different colours
Brown, orange, black and white
Each one is unique to us
Each one a beautiful sight

Each one has a story to tell
If only they could speak
Instead we piece together the puzzle
For those answers that we seek

But that is in the past now
The future is what counts
To offer safety and security
They come on leaps and bounds

Endless days spent playing
Together with their friends
A life of companionship and comfort
Their happiness never ends

We have such admiration
For the strength that each one shows
the love we feel when watching them
just blossoms as they grow

and so, it must be said
for indeed it is very true
when one finds the time to leave us
our hearts just turn to blue

we miss those who have departed
but we keep them with us still
forever etched upon our hearts
forget them? we never will

we cherish the ones who are living
and those we know have gone
and every day we send our love
with each new rising sun

another rainbow we may see
as we look up to the sky
our hearts full of love and happiness
but tears we silently cry

so, while we know we have them here
we shall indeed do our very best
to give them everything they need
this is their place to rest

to enjoy a life so wonderful
and feel loved so pure and true
each cat who comes to Torre Argentina
we love them all, yes, we do

thank you to those who care
and support us every day
without your help we cannot do
what we do in our own way

if you are coming to visit Rome
make sure you do stop by
I promise you will enjoy it here
But when you leave you may cry

Everyone is welcome here
Together we are all friends
A love for cats make friendships
Ones which cannot end

let's carry on our work today
For who knows what is in store
But one thing for sure we know is true
We cannot love our cats more

We love them from inside our souls
A love we know they feel
For here at Torre Argentina
Everything is real

We thank you all so very much
And our cats they thank you too
please say hello next time you come
they are waiting here for you

Cats of the Distance Adoption Programme

Revlon

When cats arrive to the shelter we often have some background information about them or we at least know something but one day during winter a little ginger cat arrived in the area sacred. Already sterilised and with a microchip we knew he came from a home but the microchip told us nothing and so we were left to wonder.

We can only assume that someone no longer wanted this friendly boy and had sadly left him there to fend for himself. One thing that never shocks us is just how cruel people can be and the lengths they go to when they become tired of a cat.

What was his story and who had once looked after him? Poor Revlon had been abandoned and left for us to take care of him. Of course, we welcomed him, and we knew he would easily find a home, we just had to find the best person who would fall deeply in love with him the same as we did.

In the Nursery Revlon really settled in easily but he wasn't a fan of the other cats. He loved humans but other cats not so much! He wasn't aggressive but just preferred humans and so after we knew he had been health checked and we knew he wouldn't run away he could live between the office and nursery and choose where he wanted to be like so many of our healthy cats do.

He chose the office area and became a good friend to Silvia, often sitting on her knee while she was working at the computer. Revlon showed such a sweet side to everyone that we knew he would find a home.

During his wait a tender moment occurred when a visitor came into the shelter wearing a yellow tartan plaid skirt. Something strange happened. Revlon became beside himself and we could not remove him from the girl's skirt.

Something inside him was aroused and he felt a sense which was once familiar to him. Had he once had his own plaid blanket? Was it her scent? Did she remind him of someone? Or did her skirt remind him of the home he once had and the blanket he was once happy to lie and sleep upon?

We don't know the truth of what happened but after that moment we really knew that Revlon was better suited to a happy loving home. It was nothing less that he deserved. With his sweet personality and always happy to offer his big pink belly for us to rub it didn't take much longer. Soon a new daddy came to pick him up and take him home.

We didn't have to wait long for news of Revlon and we were delighted to see beautiful photos of him lying sweetly on the sofa beside his new dad and of course with his very own plaid blanket which he will enjoy for the rest of his life.

Good things come to those who wait, and Revlon really deserved this special moment and for the ones who abandoned him then surely it is a great loss to you and for us we are at least grateful that we were able to rescue him.

Revlon will never be forgotten, happy new home!!!

Lumachina

Life is life. Life is everything that we try to enhance and sustain and encourage. In the case of Lumachina life certainly means everything.

Paralysed from the waist down yet still a fighter. Surviving by the will of god to continue in this harsh and often cruel world this girl truly deserved a chance. We offer this to her. When others may put a price on this life we did not. When others may put a value on this life we valued her life as a priceless gift. We accepted her, and we wanted her.

Some may say an she would be an inconvenience, too much trouble, or just hard work.

Yet to us it is nothing and yet she is everything.

We will do only our best and encourage her and care for her and give her endless comfort.

A sweet young baby scared and shy yet with the courage of a lion and the heart of a puppy. We will fight for you dear Lumachina to survive and live a happy life with us.

We hope you find comfort in the comfortable baskets with blankets and warmth. The food and weekend chicken parties. We hope you find friends who will be your shelter when you need it. We hope our visitors will give you the space when you are overwhelmed and the love you desire when you want it. We hope you allow us to love you for all that you are, all that you were, and we know all that you will become.

We do not know everything of Lumachina's past life before she arrived here, and many people have expressed sadness at her condition and want to know more. Our information is limited to knowing she was dragging herself around a carpark and although she is paralysed still somehow managed to escape help for quite some time.

We do not however wish to hide her away and we shall celebrate her and enjoy her for whatever time we are lucky enough to have her. She may progress and already we witnessed some small movements of her back legs and she is so clever to use the litter box areas correctly with no help!

It is true she may live for many months, years or sadly only weeks, but we cannot know what lies ahead. Already fragile, her life hangs in the balance. We wish to always be honest and true.

We will do our best as always, the same as we do for all our wonderful cats and we appreciate your support and care and most of all love for Lumachina. Believe us we will do all we can!!!

Marzapane

August 2017 had been a terrible month, many of our beloved cats had passed over the Rainbow Bridge so we welcomed this very battered cat with joy and open arms!

He had a squamous cell carcinoma in his ears and his mouth was in terrible condition, he still needed to be sterilized and, not surprisingly, he was also positive for FIV, something very common in feral un-neutered cats living in colonies or on the streets.

He arrived to us from Guidonia where he had appeared in the cat colony of a volunteer. Soon we found that he is a very nice affectionate and playful guy like our beloved Gianburrasca, a wonderful cat who had recently just left us.

Marzapane needed to visit the dentist for treatment on his teeth which were in bad condition and so gave us the perfect excuse to keep him here at the shelter with us

Lucky for us he has settled in well into Nursery life and now chooses to move between the Nursery, Office and outside depending on his mood! One of the funniest photos we found by accident of Marzapane is of him hanging off the door handle to the Nursery trying to get back in! With all his fat lumps and bumps proudly on display!!

He is very social and gets along with all the other cats. He loves to play and being a youngish boy, his nature is still very kitten like. Perhaps because he now doesn't have to worry about finding a meal or place to sleep.

Marzapane is always jumping, chasing toys and many times enjoying his greatest passion in life.... eating! He certainly is a little round and we love his chubby little belly. It always makes us smile.

He has a fondness for the ladies... and because of this he was given the title "Love Machine". He is exactly like his name Marzapane and very, very sweet!

Chestnut

Chestnut came to Torre Argentina many years ago back in the October of 2007. She has remained here ever since and because she has been such a long-term resident you could say she has become part of the furniture. A veteran and long-standing citizen.

Poor Chestnut was left inside a cat carrier at the front door of the shelter. When we arrived and found the carrier we weren't surprised to see the other contents inside. She had been abandoned but was not alone.

Inside the carrier with her were her three young kittens. The poor girl was no longer wanted but thankfully she was left with us and not on the street and so we were able to help her. One of our wonderful volunteers Daniele fostered her and the young kittens as they were still too young to enter the shelter.

When the kittens were old enough and vaccinated they entered the shelter and of course being small and sweet they quickly caught the eyes or admirers and all three of the kittens were adopted to families of their very own. Great news for them but Chestnut was just never so lucky.

Maybe Chestnut was annoyed at being left here and let us know with her grumpy, short tempered, irritable nature. As the years went on we accepted this and laughed at calling her a grumpy old lady. However, as the years went on she perhaps accepted that this was going to be her forever home and she mellowed a lot.

When she finally accepted us, and mellowed she settled well into the sanctuary life. She started to find joy in little things. Spending time outside next to the large welcome poster, catching the eye of those who were arriving. Many photos were taken of Chestnut because of this and we are sure she knew what she was doing when she chose this spot!

Now her days are spent welcoming visitors who come and is happy to be petted and given attention or affection. She will let you know though when she has had enough and it's mostly on her terms. We think she is just great and quite like her quirky character.

Bretella

A new cat to the Torre Argentina Bretella is named so because his name means Strap. This young boy was brought to us with terrible injuries to his front leg.

The victim this time not of a car but from a collar around his neck. He had once belonged to someone it seems with this identifiable object around his neck but who could leave him in such a terrible way?

It seemed he had been wandering for quite some time with this horrific wound. So long that the constant rubbing of the collar on his inside leg had caused irreparable damage to all the muscle and tissue and his leg ended up paralysed and dead.

Bretella has had to wait a long time before he has been able to have his surgery. Where the wound is situated if the amputation of the leg was to proceed too early he would be at a high risk of the wound re-opening and there is not enough skin to close it. It is very precarious and dangerous and so to avoid this we wait patiently but not as patient as Bretella.

Poor Bretella has been so easy-going waiting for his operation and never complains. We think he knows we are waiting for the right time to help him.

He is a friendly sweet boy and because of his young age he makes a great addition to the nursery. Once his operation is over and his wound healed we are sure he will find joy in playing with the many toys and other cats.

He is always happy to be touched and loves to dribble all over anyone who wants to be close to him. We are sure it is dribbles of love and happiness and we don't mind at all.

Bretella despite his hard start has great prospects and we know will be very popular with all who visit him, this sweet black panther deserves all the best.

Dreyfus

We don't know too much about this little old guy. All we know is he is around ten years old.

He arrived at the shelter after he was spotted in the colony of a young lady who kindly cares for some cats. She had spotted his eyes and noticed that they showed the classic symptoms of blindness.

She was very concerned and worried that he would be in danger if she left him to fend for himself on the streets.

He is very skinny and of course positive for FIV as many street cats are and he has taken quite some time to adjust to the life in the Nursery.

He spent most of his time at the beginning sitting at the back of the nursery on the baby pads just observing what he could and listening. It was clear from the beginning that Dreyfus isn't completely blind and can perhaps see light or shadows for he always knows when he is being approached.

Be sure to put your hand out slowly so he is not frightened, and you will see his small head come towards your hand for strokes and then listen. Right away you will be sure to hear his very loud motor purring starting as he finds great pleasure in being touched.

He is really very sweet, even if still a little shy. As time has progressed so indeed has Dreyfus and he now has chosen a bed of his own up on the back tables, close to where he feels safe but not now on the floor. He stays close to little Xoriana and perhaps they can become soul mates.

In the afternoons he likes to take a walk around the nursery, mostly around 3-4pm when it is a bit calmer and quieter. There he explores a little and smells everything around him. We are sure it won't be too long before he finds other comfort in the big cat tree beds and luxury penthouse apartments, only if Codina moves long enough to allow him a day of sleeping there or maybe just an afternoon.

He has shown real bravery in just a short time with us and its remarkable to see how these once feral cats can adapt to a new life which is so alien to their original beginnings and everything they have even known in their short lives.

Dreyfus has a great appetite and he adores chicken. Since his sight is limited he loves to have his own plate all to himself and eat at the back of the room, in his little safe area. Chicken is most likely a luxury treat for him having had such a hard life.

We hope he is enjoying his time with us for we really are happy to have him with us here in the Nursery.

Dreyfus you are a real charmer.

Rubio

A beautiful young cat with the most amazing almond shaped eyes and marble paintings on his back arrived one day back in 2015 among the ruins. We have no idea how or why. Or perhaps we do but we just can't think about it.

How could anyone not want this sweet boy?

With such a great calm and friendly character, we were sure he would become a member of his own family in no time and be packing his bags and off on his new adventures, however, fast forward several years and Rubio remains with us.

Perhaps people don't like big cats or older cats? Rubio is a beauty, that is for sure. In-fact possibly one of a kind with his amazing and unusual handsome looks and markings.

When you see Rubio lower your head to him, he will firstly give you many head bumps to let you know he is your friend and then ladies get ready for the greatest thing ever. You will have a whole new look in minutes!

Did you know that Rubio is also a hair stylist? He will perform miracles and you will leave the shelter with a whole new look as he performs his party trick of massaging your head and restyling your hair. He is quite creative, and only asks for a small tip on the way out as a contribution towards the chicken parties. Some might say that's a fair swap!

Really Rubio is very affectionate and enjoys the attention of humans, always happy to be touched and he always also looks like he is smiling.

We are happy he is now choosing to spend more time in the office where more people can see him, and he is visible. Our wonderful handsome big boy Rubio.

Zenone

Living in the cat colony of Villa Celimontana Zenone was very well and living happily. With the other cats that is.

You see Zenone had one big problem and it wasn't that he was a feral cat living in a colony. No that was the least of his problems. Is one big problem which became his real big problem was that he hated dogs.

He hated dogs with a great passion and was happy to start a war with any who passed by. Chasing them and scaring them he was living on his nerves waiting for his next victim. This may be fine when the victim is a small and innocent puppy who may be small or who thinks that Zenone just wants to play.

Zenone should have learned to choose his victims more wisely because one day he certainly made a big mistake. He chose a dog who was worldlier than he was. Hanging off the dog's neck Zenone went in with delight however the dog was having none of it and bit poor Zenone on the back leg.

The bite although not deep was still deep enough to shatter the leg and so an amputation was required to help poor Zenone. So that he didn't encounter this problem again he was brought to Torre Argentina where he could be sure he would never see another dog again. We must protect the dogs....!

He is a sweet friendly guy, on the larger side however we don't think he knows as he always chooses the smallest round bed and somehow manages to fit himself into it like a cinnamon bun! Very cute and endearing.

Zenone would make anyone smile and we hope you too when you meet him.

Stealth

Another new addition to the Nursery in 2018 is Stealth. Coming from Ciampino Stealth was again an un-sterilised cat and was most likely in search of a female.

His roaming led him into the path of a car and again he became a victim and had severe damage to his back leg. Brought to us to save not just his hind leg which had to be amputated but surely his life.

Positive for FIV as most un-sterilised male cats are, we set to work in making him welcome at the shelter, he was fixed giving him the sterilisation which was long overdue, and his amputation wounds given time to heal.

Stealth is quite a calm boy and enjoys spending a lot of time sleeping in the large baskets in front of the window.

He is always happy to share with the other cats, that is if they can find a space to park themselves for Stealth is another cat who is also on the larger side.

He is very sweet and sociable however has a fondness for our volunteer Laura. If anyone gets too close to her and he notices then something in his brain switches and he soon becomes a street ruffian, a rebel and might attack.

We know he is going to be very popular with everyone who visits, he has a delightful coloured coat, not unusual in its markings but the colour is spectacular, and he is very photogenic.

Tarek

Tarek was brought to the shelter along with his sister Tassia in 2008 when they were just four months old. A kind Gattara Sandra had spotted them in her colony and felt they had a good chance of finding a home and wanted to give them that chance they would not have otherwise had on the streets.

Since they were already four months old neither of them were very social it seemed they had missed out on the window of opportunity to be adopted.

They were destined for a life at the shelter with us. Unfortunately, Tassia passed away in 2014 and Tarek was left alone.

Over the years Tarek has mellowed slightly from his once feral self and comes to the office area for treats and has become more affectionate.

He has a loud meow and will always let you know when he is around by trying to trip you up manoeuvring in between your legs as you walk around.

He could easily be lost among the other black cats, but he had a bad reaction to his vaccination and so has some scar tissue on his lower back which can be seen and, he has two cute fangs which stand out and he looks like a mini vampire.

Tarek is a sweet boy and worthy of all our affections.

Lampadina

Rome is a city close to the sea but on the coast are lot of strays. In summer the houses are full of families living there but after holiday season the families return from their holiday homes back into the cities. Left behind are the cats fending for themselves and for some strange reason these people think the cats can survive there alone until their next visit.

Fortunately, there is a feeding association run by volunteers who collect strays, sterilise them and provide much needed care if it is required. Some will also try and rehome any cats who can be rehomed. We help this association with the sterilisations and by welcoming any disabled cats who they cannot keep and who could not survive outside on their own.

Princess Lampadina is one of these cats. A bad infection in her eyes left her totally blind. With one eye so badly damaged that our veterinarian even had to remove it she now resembles a little white pirate.

Lampadina remains healthy and eats very well. When joining the nursery, she was very shy and unsure of her surroundings. She chose to spend most of the day sleeping in a little quiet corner where she felt secure and safe. Allowing beside her the company of a little old cat called Cocoon, they were two souls who needed one another and provided the comfort each desired so much. With her always being present in this corner we even made a little sign and named it "Lampadina's corner". Her very own private quarters of her own.

Her appetite thankfully made her bold and encouraged her to venture into the centre of the nursery, her nose guiding her to the food she loved. There we would put the saucers of treats that she likes so much and protect her from the other cats who would try and steal her food. She has her own private plate at feeding time and she enjoys this very much just like a real Princess would.

Time changes most people and one might say, even cats, for now Lampadina no longer desires her private quarters and in fact sits very happily beside the door of the cage, can we say......waiting for victims? Now, this shy sweet girl knows the door of the nursery and always waits to escape, perhaps she wonders what is beyond that cage door? She sits, waits, then pounces on the legs of her victims, hanging on for dear life and especially likes the legs of our very own Monica. Using Monica's legs like a tree she is a cheeky girl now and full of fun. She loves when Monica plays with her.

Everyone who meets Princess Lampadina falls in love with this innocent and beautiful white beauty but beware when entering the nursery, she might be waiting for your legs. Just know that she loves you really.

Calibano

When Calibano arrived at the shelter he was in a terrible condition. He was found in the December of 2016 with awful injuries. He had a broken jaw and trauma to his little head which had caused him to have one displaced eye and we later found him to be completely blind. We think his injuries were most likely caused by a car.

We were not ready to give up on Calibano and started the long process of helping him and trying to nurse him back to full health. Blindness for us is nothing and we knew if he could find the fight to recover then we would stand by him and give him a good life with us.

His wonky jaw was reset so that he would be able to eat properly after recovery and his right eye was removed completely. He was only around 5 years old and we knew could live a long time. He responded to his treatment and he showed us he has a zest for life and we knew he was something special.

As time passed Calibano started to gain weight, certainly his injuries had not caused him any problems for eating with full gusto and he is always present at our famous chicken parties. Gaining a bit of weight and with his beautiful stripes on his tabby coat he now rather resembles a watermelon and with his round fuller figure this is what we often call him. Our little watermelon. We are just so glad to see him enjoying his food and knowing that he has not suffered any long-lasting effects from his jaw injury and that he did recover well.

He is named after the main character in the famous Shakespeare play the Tempest. Popular in literature and popular with all who come to the shelter. He is also very popular with the other cats and isn't very often found in a basket alone. Part of the "basket gang" he indulges in many snoozes with his friends, Grumpy, Brutus and Rafaella. They are almost always together and even if all of them are not together Calibano loves spending time with his best friend Brutus. Some say they could be twins. Although Brutus is a slightly "trimmer" version of Calibano but Brutus being deaf, and blind, seems to rely on Calibano, the ears for him.

Isn't it wonderful that they seem to reach out to those who they know can help them?

If you visit and cannot find Calibano right away, then look to the lower baskets and follow the sound of the snoring.... You will be sure to hear him before you see him!

Raffaella

Raffaella became a resident of Torre Argentina in October 2003 and is now our longest resident and this year celebrated her 15th birthday.

When she arrived, she was just a four-month-old kitten. Along with her two siblings she was found close to one of the public libraries in Rome. The Bibliotecha Raffaello and because of this they were named Biblio, Teca and Raffaella.

The kittens were sadly very sick with feline calicivirus, a highly contagious disease that affects not only the mouth and the upper respiratory organs but also the lungs. We sadly could not save Teca but Biblio and Raffaella survived. For this we were thankful.

Both took quite some time to recover and for Raffaella much longer. Biblio being still more feral than Raffaella decided the Area Sacred was the perfect place for him to live but for Raffaella she decided to stay indoors. We think this choice may have been because she spent so long inside during her recovery. Either way we were happy that she was fine again and still with us.

Sadly, Raffaella waited and waited and for some unknown reason was never adopted and so has spent her whole life with us. We are not complaining but we think it is sad that she just never caught the eye of her someone special.

She really is a beautiful girl with giant eyes, a stunning white coat and beautiful grey markings on her head which always make her look like she is surprised. She doesn't like the company of humans as much as the other cats and will happily spend many happy hours snoozing in the baskets with her friends. The basket gang made up of Calibano, Brutus and Grumpy with Raffaella the only female. We are sure the boys just enjoy making her feel like a lady and acting like her personal bodyguards and assistants.

She is very shy and recently suffered a little with poorly health, she was given fluids for around ten days and she seemed to pick up a little. We understand she is already old, but we hope she can keep going just a bit longer for we really enjoy having her with us in the Nursery and finally she is no longer the anonymous cat she once was.

Our shy sweet old lady with a lot of gumption, our lovely Raffaella.

Fabula

In February 2017 amongst the ruins of the Piazza Vittorio a little grey and white female cat appeared. Unable to know what age she was or where she had come from we just had to catch her to give her a full health check. In doing so it was found she required a sterilisation and it was discovered that she had a bad upper respiratory infection and was not able to remain in the ruins.

It was decided that a volunteer would take her to enable the process of antibiotic treatment to help her recover and fight off the infection. She responded well to the treatment and was brought back to Torre Argentina after one month. We felt she had great prospects to be adopted and this decision was better for Fabula.

We had hoped she might find a great forever home because of the many cats who are successfully adopted and that we owed her this chance in her life. However, fate works in strange ways and it seems she is destined for her life to be lived with us. For this we will not complain since she is beautiful, kind and affectionate when she chooses to be. Fabula loves to sit on the laps of the office staff when they are working on the computers and keeps their knees warm on a colder day.

Fabula is a favourite of Monica and often sits outside waiting for her to come to the shelter, so she can stay close to her, either on her knee if she is working on the admin or beside the baskets in the front office, next to the front door. We think she sits there so she can keep a close eye on Monica and if she can find a way to stop her leaving she may one day figure it out and try it.

In summer Fabula even surprised us by spending time outside close to the front entrance where the visitors would see her as they approached from the stairs. Many beautiful photographs were captured of her in the arms of many visitors, enjoying the attention and her moment to shine.

Fabula has the longest legs in the world and is so happy to wrap them around those who accept her hugs.

We think that everyday Fabulous Fabula celebrates her new life and is very grateful. She gives back so much love to those who care for her. It's sweet to see, and really what could be more beautiful in life?

Dadino

Dadino arrived at Torre Argentina in January of 2016. He came from a colony of cats who were living close to a school which had closed. The carer noticed that Dadino who had a strange eye condition was always with another cat called Bloster. It is possible that Bloster had saved little Dadino more than once from being hit by passing cars.

Bloster had become his protector however the carer knew that the situation was too precarious and dangerous and had to find a way to remove Dadino from the conditions he was living in. Dadino was brought to Torre Argentina and given the name Dadino which means "little die" with reference to the number of times his life had probably been spared.

He was given a full health check and his condition was diagnosed as third eyelid where the eye lids cover the whole eye. He can see shapes, light and moving objects so although he is not fully blind his condition still meant it was dangerous to leave him where he was. He settled into the nursery with the other cats well and enjoyed the fluffy beds and after many months of patience was happy to be stroked and handled by the volunteers and visitors.

A stunning young tuxedo cat Dadino always caught the eyes of admirers and he became known affectionately as "Little Cloudy Eyes" because of his condition. He has thin long legs with white feet which look like little boots and we always think he looks so very elegant and stylish.

We are sure all the other cats are jealous of him. He has a gracefulness surrounding him and has captured the hearts of many people. He loves now to spend time outside as well as inside and always comes back to us around 12 o clock for his lunch and some biscuits. It's so well timed we think he has a built-in clock!

If you see Dadino be sure to spend some time with him, this friendly sweet boy will steal a little piece of your heart so be warned but I am sure it is worth it.

Neronia

A few years ago, in July the summer of 2015 a little black kitten had been spotted close to the Colosseum by tourists. We have some amazing people who offer to help us and one of those is our famous Paola who did her amazing work as usual and caught the little kitten.

The little kitten was so young she was not yet able to enter the shelter and thankfully our wonderful Daniele had space for a foster and so he took her in until she was old enough to be a part of Torre Argentina.

Many young kittens even when they are feral are easily socialised and adapt well to human company. They are naturally full of fun and if given a cat toy or piece of string will happily play for hours but not Neronia. She surprised us by not wishing to be bothered by anyone at all. Not a person or a piece of string.

She was not even interested in cuddles and rejected any form of affection. After eight weeks of ignoring Daniele's affections and finally having had her vaccinations and ready to be sterilised she was brought into the shelter. It was hoped that she would catch the eye of someone being still a young kitten and for us at Torre Argentina kittens are the easiest of all the cats to find homes for.

Neronia surprised us again by never catching the eye of anyone. We thought it was because she was a black cat and people sometimes associate black cats with being unlucky but with never showing any affection or playfulness like all the other kittens were doing she was always un-noticed and simply blended into the background.

It was unfair to keep her caged so eventually knowing that she was not going to be adopted we had to release her into the main nursery with the other cats there. Many cats like Neronia prefer to go off into the ruins but she surprised all of us by staying close. She may not like us humans, but something keeps her close to us, perhaps the older cats give her some comfort that we cannot. Or perhaps she just accepts them and not us.

Neronia is easily identified by being a smallish cat, all black, except from her white dots along her back which really stand out. It is like someone took a little paint brush and gave her some polka dots of her very own. A beautiful unusual coat which makes her stand out from the other black cats and identifiable.

She is a calm girl and we think she does enjoy her life here even if she cannot find a way to tell us or show us, a true cat. Our Neronia.

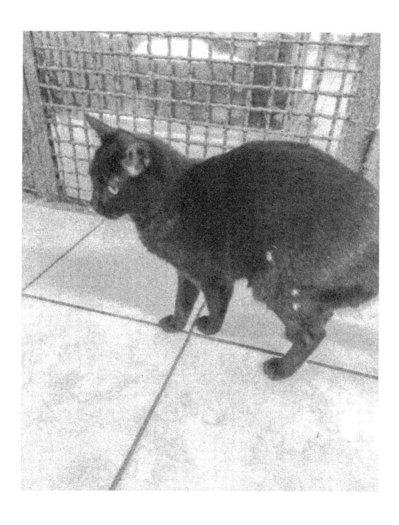

Raptus

Raptus arrived at Torre Argentina in the March of 2013. She was in a bad way when she was caught by our amazing cat catcher Paola.

At around just six months of age and still just a kitten she had a badly damaged left leg which was completely paralysed and causing her great distress.

It was decided that her quality of life would be limited if we left the leg as it was, so we made the decision with the vet that she would be able to cope fine without the leg and in fact much better without it than to leave it as it was. The amputation was arranged and due to her disability, she was a perfect candidate to become a permanent resident of the shelter.

Raptus adjusted well to having one leg less after her operation and walks a bit like a little rabbit, hopping around on her three legs. Despite being caught relatively young she remains shy and part feral, not always happy to have us humans touch her and even with only three legs she can move fast if she wants to run away from us.

We thought she might be happy to stay outside in the ruins as many of the feral cats do but despite not really liking us so much she remains close. She has built up a level of trust and perhaps she understands that we have in our own way helped her.

Poor Raptus has always wanted nothing except a true love of her own. We started to call her the black widow for every cat she ever loved passed away. Unlucky in love Raptus has never given up hope. Her first love was Pigolo, but he made it very clear to her that he was not interested in her advances. She then moved onto Skye who preferred his food bowl to poor Raptus. Finally, Raptus found her one true love in Signor Kenneth who loved her as much as she loved him. They were always together and could be seen head bumping one another in a real deep affectionate way. Sadly, Kenneth passed away and Raptus was found to be alone once more. She still sought love from our dear sweet Gottardo who also spurned her advances.

Instead spending much time hiding behind various cat flaps waiting for the opportunity to re-enter the building when it was safe.

We think she might be luckier to accept us humans for we love her unconditionally even if she does not feel the same.

Perhaps her one true love is out there somewhere, and she just has not met him yet, we hope she will find him one day. We know she certainly has not given up and we have to say, its so sweet to know that Raptus still believes in the power of love, the greatest feeling in the world so maybe she is the clever one and we should take a leaf out of her book.

Joan Collins

When you see beautiful Joan-Collins you may immediately think of a sweet fluff ball who loves to cuddle with you but don't be fooled by her outer image.

This diva came to us back in 2013 when she had attacked her owners while they were sleeping. They felt the only solution was either euthanasia or a daily dose of Prozac and so to find a way to save her life she was brought into TA with the hope that we could help her. At 5 years of age she had already been sterilised and vaccinated so this wasn't a problem, but we had to work out how best to work with her temper and diva outbursts.

To begin with she didn't take the sedatives mixed in with her meals, but we know cats love eating and soon hunger got the better of her and she started to eat. For some reason the sedatives didn't have much effect on this strong-willed lady so our attempts at being able to try and keep her calm enough to slowly socialise her failed.

After one month she was let free into the Area Sacred. For a whole month she stayed there hiding from us until one day she re-appeared. Making her own choice to remain close to us but still free she chose one of the comfortable beds in the office and made it her own.

She may have decided that she prefers the luxury life of being indoors, but she is still certainly in control of everything and makes her own rules. She has a you can look but don't touch rule that you must obey otherwise you may risk losing a limb. The rule doesn't only apply to humans, it also applies to many of the other cats too who keep a distance from danger.

If you meet Joan-Collins she is recognisable by the tattoo in her ear, a marking from when she was neutered in Paris. What a life story she has if only she could tell us! Her history of being in Paris also means she could be the only French cat in Rome. Oh-la-la!!! I think that's where her diva status comes from!

One person who did manage to overcome Joan-Collins wrath is Laura our cat-tamer and who luckily for us is able to apply sun-cream lotion onto Joan-Collins ears to prevent sun damage. White cats can suffer a lot with damage by the sun and for us this is important to protect her. If she does want to be outside in the hot summers and sunbathe she must be safe.

This diva lady is certainly not able to find another home, so we offer her up to distance adoption only because we think she would really like the celebrity status and to have many mums and dads, brothers and sisters around the world and if they stick to HER rules they will all get along just fine.

Grumpy

Grumpy was the 1094th cat brought into the Torre Argentina again by Paola our champion cat trapper in June of 2014. A little boy of four years of age he had no tail, but we do not know why or what had happened to him. He had no significant injuries apart from being in a state of neglect, very thin and having lost the sight in one of his eyes most likely due to a herpes infection which is very common in feral cats. It was no surprise when he also tested positive for FIV.

Due to him not being happy to be in the shelter he was named Grumpy because he was just that. A grumpy little man who didn't want to have anything to do with us humans.

Fast forward just nine months and he should really have been given a name change for now he is anything but grumpy! An affectionate little boy he loves to sit on visitor's knees and cuddle up to them. He craves affection, attention, is love hungry and so very sweet indeed!

Clearly his socialisation in the Nursery has done wonders. He has had a few best friends in the Nursery, sadly one being sweet Gianburrasca and Ray Charles who he misses very much. Also Grumpy is now a member of the basket gang you have heard about, with Calibano, Brutus and Raffaella, hugs on tap for Grumpy now.

Grumpy will find anything to sleep on and has a fondness for handbags as well as knees. If you leave your handbag lying on the floor on the nursery beware the moment you look its possible that Grumpy will be on top of it keeping it warm, maybe he is trying to tell you that he wants to come home with you.

We know that Grumpy would not be happy in a home where we might be left for several hours a day alone, he craves attention and affection from humans and cats alike so for him life in the nursery is the perfect situation and one which we know makes him happy every day. We don't know if there has ever been a cat who is happier than Grumpy.

Tina

Tina is a very cute feline lady who came to us here at Torre Argentina in 2013 from a colony where all the cats lived free and cared for. With each cat already sterilised the colony was perfect.

Tina was happy living there and would happily have lived there her whole life but one day the Gattara who cared for this colony found her in a bad way.

An awful accident had left her badly injured. Her tummy was torn and her intestines protruding. The kind Gattara knew she needed immediate help and rushed her to the vet. It is with no doubt that she saved her life with her quick actions.

At the vet she was given a full check-up and an X-ray confirmed she also had a broken pelvis. It is most likely that her injuries had been caused by a car. Sadly, here at Torre Argentina a lot of the disabled cats have been victims in the same way with various injuries, but Tina really was in a bad way.

It is a miracle that Tina survived this terrible accident however with the amazing care of the vet who didn't give up and the lightning reactions of the Gattara her life was saved.

Tina recovered well and is now in great shape and the scarring she was left with is her badge of courage and she wears it with pride.

She was named Tina after our wonderful volunteer Tina, the cats' very own private linen lady who has done an amazing job of taking care of the cats' baskets almost from the beginnings of life at TA.

Life in the shelter was then very different and the underground space was freezing cold in winter and very hot and humid in summer Tina's baskets were lined with wool in winter and cotton in summer making sure our feline friends felt safe and for most it was a luxury they had never had before.

Besides sharing the same name, the human and feline Tina have something in common too, both just never stop talking. It makes us laugh with joyfulness as it is endearing, sweet and fun in both the cat and human version of Tina.

Recently Tina suffered another health scare where we thought she had cancer. It was positive news for her and she just needed some extra care and ointments and the results were negative for cancer. What a relief.

Tina after all she has been through deserves a full and rich life here with us and we hope she will be here a long time.

Posiedone

Hello everybody I am Posiedone and I arrived at the Torre Argentina recently in August this year of 2017. So, you could call me the new kid on the block.

I was very lucky because a kind tourist found me in a yard when I was very disorientated and in fact they tell me now I am what humans call blind. My ears were in bad shape as the sun had caused cancer and it was terribly painful for me.

I was already sterilised, so someone once had taken care of me, but I don't know how or why I found myself in this situation, alone, blind and with cancer on my ears. Maybe my owner didn't want me anymore and left me in that yard, or maybe I came from a colony and had somehow become lost, I just don't remember.

I know I am a good boy and I know I have a kind heart too and everyone told me that it's very sad that this happened to me.

When the lovely volunteers at the Torre Argentina took me to the vet I immediately felt better as they took away the bad parts of my ears and I understood quickly that they were helping me. They gave me delicious food and talked to me in soft voices, so I knew they were kind and I could trust them.

I've met a lot of new people since being here, one lady is called Monica and she is nice. She looks after me well. She whispered into my ear to tell me about a chicken party that happens on a Sunday and I can't wait to attend.

Recently I was allowed out of my cage to join the others in the special nursery for the first time. I had finished my treatment, so it was now safe for me to join everybody.

I felt safe because Monica was with me the whole time. She took a video of me so that everyone could remember that special moment. I really felt like a famous movie star. I heard whispers coming from the humans that I am very much like another little boy.

They say his name was Gianburrasca and that he passed away recently, just as I arrived.

I really think they miss him a lot. They say I am like him because I'm also sweet, very loving, I like hugs and I'm a good kind boy.

I think he was very famous.

I feel so honoured that they feel this way because it seems he was very special, and I hope everyone will love me too the way they love Gianburrasca. If you come to visit me I will be waiting with endless hugs and I hope that you will fall in love with me too.

Lui

If you have ever had the pleasure of meeting Lui you probably heard him before you saw him. You could say he really likes the sound of his own voice. A chattering little boy who is very vocal and doesn't hold back.

If only we could understand what he was talking about, we just hope it is polite and friendly!

Lui arrived at the Torre Argentina in July of 2008 and is one of our long-term residents. An older gentleman now and beautiful with his black shiny coat and very friendly.

In fact, Lui is so friendly that it is just that which shaped his future. He came from a small colony of cats which was looked after by Francesca one of our lovely volunteers. The colony lived close to a railway track and she worried many times about the precarious situation they faced in that vicinity. Since Lui was so friendly she felt he could easily adapt to a life in a home and so pleaded with her father to allow him to come home with her and he finally agreed.

When Lui arrived at Francesca's home he was like a child in a toy store. So many glorious things he had never seen before. He went on a mission to destroy anything he could get his paws and claws into.

The smells, sights, sounds and objects must have been overwhelming for him and his senses were on overload. Francesca's father didn't know what to do and he knew he couldn't put Lui back into the colony after being away for so long.

He brought Lui to Torre Argentina in the hope that we could keep him here. With scratch posts all around him he is happy to sharpen his claws on those and we don't mind what he destroys if he is happy, just don't leave your items lying around if he is close by because we cannot be responsible for his actions. Maybe we should put a little warning sign on him.

Lui's name means "He" in Italian and we think it actually means "he who destroys things" but Lui would not be Lui without his fun character and troublesome side.

If you are looking for Lui and can't hear him first then look for the black cat with one white whisker, yes, one white whisker. This is also one of his other distinguishing features and we think makes him rather unique. He will be sure to give you much love and many cuddles. Our chattering little Lui.

Smemorina

Smemorina means "forgetful" in Italian and her name goes some way to telling a little of her history and how she came to be a permanent resident of the TA.

In 2015 she suddenly appeared in a colony and was quickly brought to the shelter because of the bad condition she was in. She had a badly damaged head which we think may have been the result of a car accident. Her little jaw was a wonky and her right eye protruded from her head, she had nerve damage and we think perhaps some memory loss. Therefore, we gave her the name Smemorina.

Smemorina is a Persian cat and it is unusual to find pedigree cats in colonies, so it is possible that Smemorina had become lost because of the accident. She was thankfully already sterilised and because of this we assume she really had once had a home of her own.

The damage to her jaw made it difficult for Smemorina to groom herself and her coat needed some extra care and attention. It took a lot of time and patience but bit by bit the amazing volunteers started to work on her coat and shaved her a bit at a time to allow her new fur to grow back slowly and in great condition with no lumps, bumps or matted bits.

With her fur restored to its true original glory Smemorina became a sight to behold. A real Persian Queen.

Smemorina is a very friendly girl who enjoys food, probably more than any of the other cats. Where there is food just look for Smemorina and she is sure to be there. Her wonky jaw doesn't stop her ferocious appetite. She particularly loves the chicken parties and makes sure she always has second helpings of what is on offer.

We know she had a hard time when she found herself on the streets and can only imagine what trauma she has gone through, having once had a home of her own. It must have been a shock, never mind the upset of the accident she suffered.

She has a fondness for running water and whenever she sees or hears running water she runs to it faster than the running water. She loves water so much she stands at the window which opens and meows loudly waiting for someone to come with a small watering can. She laps the water like it is a special champagne and she is in heaven.

She recently was given her very own private fountain in the nursery which allows her to have access to the running water she loves so much. All the other cats were joining in, so we had to have a second one put in place.

Smemorina also loves the yoghurt treats which she was given when she went through a period of not being too well earlier in 2018. She started to really enjoy these treats and now will follow people around the room waiting for a lick of one if she smells them.

We know that she has already stolen the hearts of many because she is just so sweet and delightful. We feel very lucky to have her here with us in the nursery where we can look at her cheeky little face every day. Smemorina is very popular by all who meet her and gives the best teddy bear hugs, wrapping his cute feet around your shoulders so if you stop by make sure you find her in the nursery. She will be waiting.

Faberge

You can easily recognise Faberge from his odd quirky crooked smile. Unfortunately, again the victim of being hit by a car. The accident sadly caused Faberge to suffer a broken right paw and of course gave him his memorable smile.

Another distinctive feature of Faberge is his striking red coat, he is beautiful. With his coat the colours of glowing red embers on a fire or reflecting off a hot sun he really stands out from the crowd.

He is very photogenic, but he knows it.

Faberge is not so attractive when he is eating and because of his wonky jaw he really should wear a napkin around his neck for he has food everywhere and all over his face. This doesn't deter him, and he has made it his mission in life to empty every food bowl around.

He is often seen or indeed photographed by passers-by when he is sitting outside close to the entrance. There he is happy to welcome guests and bask in the hot Roman sunshine holding his nose up to the air smelling all around him in the majestical way that only Faberge can.

Being an elderly boy, he is very calm and so settled well to the life at the shelter and is happy. He did decide that he enjoys the company of our dear friend Roberta who owns the shoe store close by and often Faberge makes his way there to visit her. It's a very sweet relationship they have together and one full of love and trust. We are happy that he found a friend who loves him, this is truly what he deserves. Our very own Mr Regal, Mr Faberge.

Quinoa

Stuck inside a dumpster this middle-aged boy was lucky to have been spotted by someone who called for our help in getting him out. The poor boy must have been so hungry and was looking for food

Even though his mouth was covered in sores he still wanted to eat, and this told us he was starving and most likely had been a long time since his last meal. Poor Quinoa. It was no surprise that he tested positive for FIV as his mouth and gums displayed the classic symptoms of this

He was very thin, bedraggled and his long coat was matted and uncared for. I guess with a mouth so painful grooming wasn't a high priority for little Quinoa. Who could blame him. Life must have been a game of survival for him, just trying to make it from one day to the next.

He was brought to us in 2015 and we think he could now be around 8-9 years of age. Quinoa had to have 7 of his teeth removed but this has never stopped him eating and he enjoys food very much. So much that he joins the first chicken party in the office area then sneaks into the nursery for the second chicken party and he thinks no one notices! Naughty Quinoa.

His coat was fixed slowly a little bit at a time and he is now happy to spend hours self-grooming showing off his beautiful long black and white fur to everyone.

He is also making up for lost time, using every opportunity to have some "play time" and now he can often be seen in the Nursery picking up small balls and tossing them into the air again and again. Now he can relax since he isn't spending his days searching for food or a place to sleep.

He acquired the name King Quinoa because of his large friendly presence and we think it suits him very well.

Tichiro

An unexpected snowfall graced the streets of Rome in 2012. During the snowfall found all alone was a beautiful Siamese tabby point.

Sitting gracefully next to the metro stop.

Where had he come from, was he left there, was he lost?

We didn't know any of the answers to our questions, so we took him to be checked by the vets. After a full medical examination, we were told that Tichiro was around 10 years old. One of the strange things about Tichiro was that at the age he was still un-neutered but also negative for FIV. This was extremely unusual, but even more unusual in an un-neutered cat of that age and so we can only imagine that he had been an indoor cat and had once had a home of his own.

We didn't know how he could have become so lost and set to work by putting up fliers to try and locate the owners, but no one claimed him. How sad for Tichiro.

Tichiro was friendly from the moment he saw us, and trusted humans and we thought he would soon find a new family to take him home and love him just as he once had known but it was sadly not meant to be.

Fast forward many years later and Tichiro is still with us waiting however we are happy to have him here with us.

Our wonderful Tichiro, our snow cat, our old toothless gentleman we love you for you always makes us smile!

Ray-Charles

If there was a definition for our wonderful Ray-Charles it would be "Love-Monster" He is loved by everyone who meets him.

If only he could talk and tell us his story. He cannot and so we wonder, and we simply fill in the blanks with whatever we want to.

What we do know is that one day he appeared in a colony of cats, he was completely blind but strangely neutered. This was extremely unusual and almost never heard of.

Had he once had a home? was he left there at the colony on purpose? was he lost? was he abandoned? or was he no longer wanted? Did anyone even look for him or try to find him? Despite putting up some posters in the area close to where he was found no one came forward.

Poor Ray-Charles. It must have been an awful shock for him to suddenly find himself outside in a strange place wondering what he had done to deserve this kind of treatment.

We knew he was special, we could see it from the start, and we would do whatever it took to give him the best life with us. Despite being completely blind Ray-Charles didn't let anything stand in his way and especially if that way meant fun!

Navigating the nursery was easy for Ray-Charles, perhaps because he had once lived in a home and so was used to furniture and objects being placed in the space he once knew. Quickly he memorised where everything was and could even climb up to the highest beds in the nursery as if he had full sight.

A real little ninja, he soon became known as the TA ninja cat always jumping from bed to bed, climbing on the trolleys and is always happy to play and have fun. When the fun is over Ray-Charles is happy to sleep inside the cosy beds and loves the company of the other cats too. Often sharing a bed with his friends Grumpy and Dadino.

Yokohama

In Autumn of 2015 Yokohama was found in the colony of one of our volunteers. Along with her other 3 brothers and sisters. All of them were young kittens and only a few months old. Knowing that they would perish if they were left there without a mother to take care of them lovely Valentina kindly fostered them.

When they were old enough to be brought to the shelter they received their vaccinations and all of them were sterilised. Yokohama's siblings were quickly chosen to go to a home of their own but sadly Yokohama was left on her own.

Yokohama was a bit crazy with an unfriendly nature and her feral beginnings had left her rather wild if you approached or tried to touch her. People looking to adopt a new kitten would not like this at all.

However, after a while Yokohama has mellowed and although she can sometimes be a bit unpredictable she does allow you to stroke her a little and as time goes by she does enjoy this more and more.

This year her health was not too good, and she spent some time in a cage receiving treatments, because of this she has grown to really dislike our very own Daniele, running away from him whenever she sees him. She only remembers him giving her the medications and not that he was trying to help her. Thankfully she has made a full recovery and is now back to her old healthy self.

She is easily recognisable for her black and white stripes which are rather stunning, wrapped around her like ribbons. She is a pretty girl and wears an unusual mask which has produced the name for her of the Zorro cat, the cat with the mask. She is rather voluptuous and flies the flag high for curvy ladies all over the world, a real plus size lady and proud!

Gottardo

Gottardo means "Strong" and this name is perfect to describe exactly all the trauma and heartache this young boy has gone through in his short life.

Another victim of traffic, Gottardo was hit by a car and when the vet examined him he told us the trauma to his head has caused him to now be blind. The vet surprised us by telling us that although he was now blind he was hopeful that his sight could return.

Gottardo really proved to be strong and a true fighter for as the vet predicted his sight did return and he made a full recovery.

We don't know about Gottardo's life before he arrived at the Torre Argentina, but we do know he had once had a home of his own. We know this because he must have suffered from either kidney stones or gall bladder problems and to help him his owners had allowed a procedure to be carried out to alleviate his symptoms and relieve him from pain.

Gottardo had been given a medical procedure to remove his little manhood and create an opening from which he could pee with no pain or further problems, we now had our own real-life free willy with us in the shelter.

When he was free in the nursery Gottardo became aggressive towards the other cats, possibly because he felt shocked by suddenly seeing the number of cats around when his eyesight returned.

He soon found an arch enemy in the shape of poor Tau-Fau. However, using his intelligence Tau-Fau soon learnt to stay away from Gottardo. Being the naughty boy that he is Gottardo would spend lots of time looking for him to torment poor Tau-Fau.

Gottardo can mainly be spotted in the office and enjoys the company of humans a lot! Lucky for us because it means we get to spend many hours every day with him.

He is always happy to greet visitors and even happier to spend time outside sunbathing. So much so that last summer he spent far too much time in the warm sun and got sunstroke.

He forgot to come back inside to the shade when it became too hot. Those who have visited in the middle of summer know just how warm it can be.

We had to bring him inside and put him into a cage with fluids to rehydrate him, so he could recover and from then onwards we had to keep a vigilant eye on him to make sure he didn't do it again. Silvia called him a real dummy cat for his foolish behaviour.

Gottardo loves to dress up for Christmas and he has a special Christmas Scarf that he wears with pride. He is so handsome, and it really suits him. A very stylish gentleman indeed!

Orobello

Another kitten found by a Gattara in 2007 at a metro station Orobello was only two months old. The poor boy had terrible ear mites and was brought to the TA for safety and care.

Orobello was vaccinated and sterilized and was so lucky to be adopted just two months later.

Why then is he still living at the shelter? Well Orobello's owners soon found that he was not exactly easy to train. He refused to use his litter box and instead chose to go to the bathroom wherever he wanted.

Hoping it was not a serious problem they didn't worry too much to begin with, but it didn't stop. As Orobello grew older his naughty behaviour carried on and nothing they did helped. He was given behaviour therapy, different remedies and for five whole years the family tried everything they could, but nothing was successful.

Having lost count of the endless beds, carpets, rugs Orobello had managed to ruin during his time with them with heavy hearts they decided to bring Orobello back to Torre Argentina.

It was not easy for them at all, they loved him so much, but they could not take any more.

Our nursery is at least cat proofed and we can tolerate anything here. It was very traumatic for poor Orobello to adapt to his new surroundings, he was sick with a cold and did not want to eat.

That is all behind him now and he is free from the Nursery and enjoys a quiet life lying mostly beside the merchandise. He is happy to have a stroke off visitors and has a sweet meow sound he makes as if to say to everyone "here I am"

Orobello always looks like he is sad and never happy, which makes him quite a memorable cat if he does catch your eye. Like the famous Grumpy Cat we think he is really cute.

And finally, the funniest thing about Orobello is that since he came back to the shelter he has always used the litter boxes with no hesitation whatsoever.

For Orobello despite being handsome and affectionate we know not everyone will be willing to take a chance on him so for us we are happy to have him with us in the shelter for life.

Isabeau

Isabeau was part of the colony cared for by one of our volunteers Christiana and she lived very well there. She had a noticeable defect on her front paw and we do not know what happened to it, whether it was a birth defect or whether she was involved in an unfortunate accident.

Isabeau became quite sick with a bad ear infection and was not able to receive the appropriate treatment if she was left in the colony so Cristiana brought her to the shelter.

When she arrived, she was given a full health check and we discovered she was FIV positive like many of the feral cats who had been left unsterilized for some time before a Gattara is able to organise it.

These cats again highlight how important our sterilisation programme is to prevent more cats from becoming FIV positive and as well as unnecessary breeding. Avoiding more cats and kittens from a tough life on the streets.

Isabeau now suffers chronic ear infections randomly but we can treat her. She is also now deaf because of the condition.

As if all of that wasn't enough for poor Isabeau she was found to have breast cancer which was removed with surgery but sometimes this type of cancer can return so we keep her here with regular checks to ensure it doesn't come back and if it does we would do all we can to remove or treat it.

Isabeau doesn't always enjoy receiving her medication but she really does enjoy the caresses from the many visitors who come to the shelter, always offering her belly for rubs and kisses. She is a sweet lady and although she can be shy she loves human company.

Enjoying some one-to-one attention makes her very happy and we think it's nothing less than she deserves for all she has gone through.

Maggiolina & Eusebio

If you are reading this, you may already know Maggiolina. If you don't then if we were to show you a photograph of her then we are 99% certain that you would recognise her even if you did not know her name.

Our most famous cat in the shelter Maggiolina is an "outside" cat who chooses to live free in the Area Sacred. She has her own place outside on the wall and happily sits there for many hours in the warm sunshine.

Since she spends so much time there many people often spot her before they spot any other cat or even before they realise there is a cat shelter in the vicinity. She is famous worldwide and our most photographed cat. On google searches it is always Maggiolina who will be one of the first images to pop up.

Maggiolina is so pretty and photogenic that is it not at all surprising and we say she is a target of the tourist paparazzi. A star and she has gained the title of "Queen Maggiolina" because of her somewhat regal standing.

When she arrived, we were sure she would immediately be adopted. With her beautiful unusual colours and fluffy coat, we felt it would not take long however still she remains with us.

Maggiolina is missing a little part of her paw from an accident and has a funny little walk which you can easily spot but it doesn't hold her back from strutting on her catwalk and jumping wherever she wants to be.

Always happy to see visitors but she keeps a distance from the nursery, office and of course the volunteers. She gets everything she needs from all the tourists who come and spot her. Accepting love when she wants it and keeping a distance when she doesn't feel in the mood to be fussed over.

If you spot Maggiolina then you can be sure that another cat is not too far behind.

This beautiful brown and white male cat is Eusebio.

Always together, they are best friends. Eusebio has only three legs and hops around but is never too far from her side.

Eusebio became famous in 2018 for becoming the "google cat". An overnight sensation and a viral hit! On google if you drill down into the street view of the Torre Argentina a cat's head pops up and it is our dear sweet Eusebio.

Perhaps he knew what he was doing and wanted to become as famous as Maggiolina, his Queen. A great cunning plan!

If you spot Maggiolina and Eusebio, then be sure to look for the gentleman who is also close by. Or perhaps you may even spot them both sitting on his knee or being held in his arms like two little babies.

This gentleman is Mauro. He comes to visit them every single day. He helps us a lot because he can reach the cats outside who won't come near the volunteers. If any of the outside cats are sick or need help he can let us know. He is our outside eyes.

When you see the three of them together you will really understand what a true love is. The relationship they have together will take your breath away. It is quite something special to read about but even more special to witness in real life. Take a moment to enjoy it. They have a trust and precious bond without words, its deeper than any words could ever be and comes from the heart.

How lucky for Maggiolina and Eusebio to have their own human guardian.

Porthos

In July 2013 Porthos arrived from a colony of cats who were living in the outskirts of Rome. He came with a bad herpes infection in his eyes. Fortunately, we were able to save one eye, but he ended up blind in the other.

At the shelter he received the best medication for his condition and the virus was controlled. Due to the problem with his eye we felt it was unsafe to return him to the colony and so his life at Torre Argentina began.

We set up a place for him in the Nursery but Porthos hated it. He let us know every day just how much, making a fuss. When he was released he went straight into the Area Sacred and we thought we would be lucky to see him again. He had enough of those nasty eye drops!

For a few months he stayed away from us and we could only see him every now and again outside wandering among the ruins enjoying his solitary life. We were at least happy that he was free, and we knew he was safe, so we didn't worry too much.

After one-year Porthos started to slowly make his way back to the little garden area we have outside. A little closer each day, watching everything, perhaps making his mind up on whether it was a good idea or not. When he did finally make it close enough he made sure he still had an escape route so that if he wanted to run away he could.

Porthos now spends his time by the large stairwell and balustrade area guarding it. He is our patrol cat. Our little security man.

He now allows visitors and passers-by to stroke him and give him some cuddles but if any of the volunteers come close to him then he will run away so fast he is like a lightning bolt.

This summer we noticed he was becoming rather thin, and we wanted to bring him into the shelter for tests to make sure that he didn't have any medical issues and so we had to be creative and come up with a plan.

The volunteers removed their aprons and put on sunglasses, they put their mobiles and cameras into their hands and approached him slowly. Pretending to be tourists he was happy to allow them to stroke him. Then with a crafty quick swoop we were able to catch him and gather him inside for his tests which were thankfully normal. It may be that he was just suffering from the summer heat when the cats become lazy, not eating as much and when some of the cats do become thinner.

Now Porthos will come into the shelter when the chicken parties are in full swing. He doesn't stay long but he stays long enough for us to say hello and for him to know we provide good treats and that he doesn't have to be scared anymore.

Brutus

Gattara are special and never fail to notice cats in need. Brutus was very lucky when he was spotted. He was not in good condition at all. Missing an eye but also suspected to be blind in the other she took him to the vet to be checked. Poor Brutus, as well as being blind he was confirmed as being deaf.

Estimated to be juts three years old it wasn't a surprise to us that he also tested positive for FIV like many un-sterilised male cats. He had most likely been seeking females for some time.

However, knowing he had actively chased females we knew his injuries couldn't have been from birth and could only have been caused by a blow from a car or motorbike. His accident had clearly caused his injuries and we knew he would have been unable to survive on the streets in the bad condition he was in.

He was brought to Torre Argentina and because he was such a feral cat on the outside he was used to keeping a safe distance from humans. Now inside and with no eyes or ears to understand what was going on around him Brutus was in shock.

He found some security in one of our cat tree houses and with the company of another cat just like him. "Lady Macbeth". It is possible with both being so feral that they understood they needed to help one another to adjust and to once again enjoy life.

Through time both improved building up the confidence to leave their "house" but Brutus took a lot longer. Initially wary of humans he preferred the company of other cats finding a friend in Gollum. Sadly, Gollum decided to move to the Area Sacred and left poor Brutus behind.

Being blind and deaf Brutus was unable to join him and remains in the nursery however there are many other friends to find comfort with and Brutus became a member of the basket gang with sweet Grumpy, Watermelon Calibano and Old Lady Raffaella.

Brutus has come a long way from his days on the street and despite having no sight he has been seen playing with little toy balls. A huge step for a tom cat from the streets and one which gives us immense pleasure to see.

Brutus now enjoys the caresses of humans and is a sweet boy, he has a big kind heart and with everything he has overcome in life we know he deserves the very best in life and we do everything we can for him to make it so.

Ivanka

There is sugar and there is spice and there are lots of things nice and then there is Ivanka.

A unique cat and certainly with a fiery individual character and strong independent personality we do not know what happened to her.

A young cat she found all alone crying on the street by a gentleman who brought her to us. He assured us she was sweet and full of fun and we thought with the vaccinations and sterilisation she would be a perfect candidate to be adopted.

Perhaps this man knew the truth and had us all fooled?

For Ivanka turned into a monster at the shelter.

She was so bad that a dividing plate had to be installed in her cage each time it needed cleaning. She was hissing and screaming at us and we don't know what she could have been saying but you can be sure whatever it was that even if we knew we wouldn't be able to tell you.

Once she could be free we hoped she would run away into the Area Sacred and leave us in peace but "sweet" Ivanka had other ideas.

No, she did not want to do this.

She had her own ideas of what she wanted. She chose to stay by the office and keep a close eye on all of us. The volunteers working in the office were terrified to move when she was sitting beside them, using any object they could find as a barrier between them and her. She acted like a guard scrutinising their every move, Ivanka took her job very seriously indeed.

Perhaps she was enjoying some revenge for being brought to the shelter. Or perhaps she really loved us but didn't know how to express it?

The only person who has been able to break down the barrier and receive some love from Ivanka is Silvia V who has a special relationship with her. Ivanka climbs onto her and sucks at her neck like a kitten to her mother. It is possible she was removed from her mother too early when she was kitten and it has caused some emotional damage. She wants to love so much but doesn't know how to control her feelings.

She is a stunning cat with the most beautiful markings and photogenic. She looks like an angel and sometimes she can be but don't be taken for a fool. Over the years she has mellowed a lot but do beware, she does like the odd bite and scratch as Silvia Z will tell you after a month of antibiotics when she used her arm in the way that a vampire would.

Ivanka really is a free spirit and if anyone knows how to tame her then let us know the secret and until then we will love her from a distance, just to be safe.

Paoletto

Sweet Paoletto turned up at the colony of our wonderful Cristiana. He had a bad limp and she was concerned about him.

She brought him to the vet for examination and they discovered that he had a semi paralysis in his left leg. There was not a requirement for an amputation as Paoletto was not dragging his leg and when he walked he was able to put his paw on the ground.

Despite keeping his leg, he was still not safe to be returned to the streets and so it was decided it would be best if he came to Torre Argentina. He was neutered and vaccinated and when tested he was found to be negative for FIV. It is very likely that this unfortunate accident had probably saved his life.

He was not left to become a frisky unneutered cat living a feral life and had been caught before any long-term damage had been done and for Paoletto it seemed he had a good future ahead and a great chance to be adopted.

He is friendly and sweet but sadly never caught the eye of his someone special.

He did catch the eye of one special lady. Our sweet little Foti who was in the nursery at the same time as Paoletto and so became a love story. Always side by side and together curled up in their little cat house it was difficult to see where one cat started and the other ended. Unfortunately, Foti became sick and she passed away in the summer of 2017.

Paoletto was left alone without his true love and decided that he wanted to be free from the life in the Nursery. He went to live in the Area Sacred only stopping by every now and again when he felt like it.

That was until some new arrivals caught his eye. A group of kittens were rescued and kept at the shelter waiting for adoption. With one of the kittens remaining rather feral and having been unsuccessful in finding a home of her own she was also set free. Lutezia a beautiful young girl has caught his eye and we watch them slowly fall in love. They are often together and enjoy head bumps and rubs of affection.

Paoletto now stays closer to the office once again because of Lutezia and we are so happy that he has once again found a friend to love because we know how much he really missed Foti.

Paoletto being a black and white cat can easily fade into the background and not stand out among the other cats, but you will easily identify him with his little black moustache and he looks like he is wearing a white top over a black sweater. He is a beautiful boy and we are very happy to have him here with us at the shelter.

Pioppo

When a beautiful grey blue cat was seen limping on three legs dragging his tail and hind leg behind him someone contacted Cristiana one of our volunteers.

Caring for a colony in the area she was the first port of call for any cats who were spotted needing help! She recognised immediately on seeing Pioppo that his leg was beyond repair and it could not be saved, and his tail was so badly damaged she knew he would also lose it.

Pioppo went through an amputation of his tail and at the same time his badly damaged leg. At the same time, he was also neutered. Pioppo was another FIV cat due to his feral background and lack of sterilisation.

His recovery was a long process because his stitches kept bursting open. Three times he was operated on to try and help his wounds heal. Due to the location of the wound he didn't have enough skin for the wound to heal easily and the slightest movement meant he faced the same problem of the stitches popping open.

It was a terrible time for Pioppo but also for poor Monica who once found him covered in blood one day, dying, because of his wound and rushed him to the vet. It was a miracle that he survived. With the amazing care of the volunteers and vets and his own will to live Pioppo thankfully made a full recovery and we named him Pioppo.

Pioppo means Poplar like the tree, he was not named this because he is tall and thin, he is in fact the opposite, small and chunky but to us he was strong and had a will to live and survive so it was perfect.

Once Pioppo made his full recovery he could be free, but he somehow understood that he must stay within the office area and not venture too far from us.

He doesn't go too far but when he is outside he enjoys time sitting on the wall stretching in all sorts of funny positions. We always laugh because it looks like he is performing a morning yoga class of his own. Staying fit and nimble or perhaps he is just showing off to all the ladies.

Pioppo is a very sweet guy and when he chooses to sleep in the beds in the office he loves the attention he receives. He has a beautiful unusual coloured coat which makes him stand out and he is very affectionate. If you sit on the floor and he is walking past, he would love to enjoy a cuddle sitting on your knee.

After all he has gone through this is the very least he deserves. We hope Pioppo is now enjoying a wonderful life with us. Our Mr Calm, our Zen guy, our wonderful little Pioppo.

Trilly

There are crazy cat ladies and there are crazy cats! No, I am not talking about Ivanka. I am talking about Trilly.

A lady rescued Trilly from the street when she saw her and fell in love with her beautiful white coat and thought she was a fragile little angel.

When she took Trilly back home with her she quickly realised that she was indeed a devil disguised as an angel and there was certainly no halo gracing Trilly's head.

Trilly was anything but grateful to be rescued and was determined to attack the poor lady and set about a tirade of bites and scratches. The lady tried everything to win Trilly over but no matter what she did Trilly was not happy.

With Trilly so clearly scared and angry she felt it was unfair to keep her there against her will and since she could not put her back on the streets she brought is to Torre Argentina.

She arrived in 2014 and has surprisingly settled in well to life with us. She seems peaceful and is a favourite of Daniele who even has a private bed set up for Trilly with her name on it and love hearts on the name tag, a sweet gesture.

Trilly is much more relaxed and falls in love with every male volunteer but for some reason she dislikes all the ladies. Perhaps they remind her of the poor woman who was so kind to rescue her and she feels threatened. We don't know but certainly if you are a male then Trilly will bestow her love upon you.

For the rest of us we take what we can get and although Trilly accepts affection it is on her terms and she will let you know when she has had enough.

Jubilee

Beautiful Jubilee was brought to the shelter when she was just 4 months old together with her whole family, except her unknown father of course.

Her mother and the three kittens were rescued from a home where they were not receiving proper care. A sad start to life for this beautiful family.

Their kind rescuer made sure that all four cats were sterilised before bringing them to safety at the shelter to live with us.

Jubilee's mother and two siblings were very affectionate and soon found a home, but picky Jubilee never found the human she looked for.

She has only ever known her life to be at Torre Argentina among the ruins however in recent years she has found solace within the nursery.

Now a teenager or some might say an older lady at the ripe old age of sixteen and a half she has most definitely enjoyed a wonderful long life with us here!

Such a beautiful girl with a beautiful blue coat she is almost oriental in her features. She's been here so long she is part of the furniture.

Quiet and unassuming she is often overlooked for the other cats, but she deserves her moment to shine like all the others!

Zebra

Poor Zebra had a tough start in life and sadly it continued. Arriving into the shelter at just one month old as a cute kitten she soon found a home through adoption but sadly was brought back after three years with the reason being she was not using her litter tray.

Poor Zebra! She waited patiently for another two years and she was lucky to be adopted again! Could this adoption be her happy ever after? No, it was not... just twelve days later she was back at the shelter with no real reason for her return.

Poor Zebra was so mixed up being taken to a new home and brought back so many times! Another ten days passed, and she was again adopted... we hoped this time for long term.... but five and a half years later Zebra was brought back to us. We couldn't believe it! This time her owner had developed an allergy and could not keep her.

When the situation could not become any worse for poor Zebra she was diagnosed as being diabetic and needed insulin every day. She also should be on a special diet to prevent her eating food that she shouldn't but that would mean she would have to be kept in a cage and it is not something we would be happy to do!

She loves to eat everything she shouldn't! Stealing lunch from the volunteers... her favourites are spaghetti and vegan falafels... a real variety of foods!!! Naughty Zebra!

A real home is what she needs so that her diet could be controlled but due to her history it would have to be a special home where she would not be returned and unsettled again! In the meantime, we are happy to have her here and we know we will never let her down!

We want to show her that it is ok to be here, and she is loved! After such a traumatic life she is better to remain settled here and loved from afar!

Frisbee

How amazing when it is the end of an era and a volunteer of the shelter helped a Gattara in trapping the last three old cats in her colony. The Gattara kindly offered to take the last three cats' home and take care of them for the end of their lives.

The end of the colony... or was it?? During the final clearing up of the area the volunteer came across a new arrival... a mother cat and four kittens hiding in the bushes!

Knowing she could not leave her there she brought them to the shelter. One of these kittens was named Frisbee. The mother cat went into a rage when she was separated from her babies but when she was with them she remained sweet and calm

This behaviour soon earned her an adoption and she left for her own forever home! The kittens however showed no signs of mellowing like their mother did and were not social at all! As soon as they could be they were released and found their freedom in the Area Sacred like many of the other feral cats.

Of the four kittens one disappeared and only two remain in the Area Sacred and Frisbee was the only one to return to the inside. He is happy inside the nursery and office area meeting and greeting the visitors.

After all he has gone through in his traumatic start in life we hope he finds some solace and calmness with us as well as endless supplies of love and chicken parties.

Genziana

When it's cold outside in the middle of winter many stray cats like to find a warm place and that warm place is often under the hood of a car!

That place was exactly where little Genziana chose to find some warmth one winter. Luckily a passer-by heard noises from the car and discovered that a tiny kitten needed help!

The kitten seeking heat had climbed in and become stuck.

Some food was placed under the car to try and attract the young kitten and it worked for soon with a wriggle or two she was finally free! The Gattara rescuer fostered the young kitten until she was old enough to come to the shelter.

She was named Genziana, but she wasn't cute or cuddly at all. She still has not found a home and although doesn't mind the odd stroke she can tell you very firmly when she has had enough.

She is a very pretty girl, almost like a female Gottardo with her colours and markings and the most beautiful eyes a cat could be so lucky to have. A deep blue green like two oceans.

Genziana can often be seen enjoying the freedom of the outside lying in the warmth of the sun! Sharing the flowerpots with her friend Disturbia.

Genziana is known as the glamour girl of Torre Argentina because of her glamorous looks and she seems happy here, at least now she does not seek car engines to go inside! We know she's safe now at the TA.

Narcisco

Some people take pity upon animals and often a great example of this is the endless work of the Gattara.

In the story of Narciso this is exactly what happened. A Gattara with a kind heart saw Narciso had a badly damaged eye due to a herpes infection. As is often the case with feral cats the infection can come from their own mothers.

She fostered the young kitten and kept him until he was vaccinated and old enough to become a resident of the TA. For sure the kind hearted Gattara had planned Narcisco's future with precise detail!

She told us she was sure the young friendly and affectionate boy would find a forever home and he did.... with us here at the TA!

He was not at all friendly or affectionate, but part of his problem is his shyness and we know he is trying to overcome this to allow him the freedom to be close to people and experience the love that they wish to share with him.

Narcisco decided to live in the Area Sacred like many of the other feral cats do and there he found a love in his friend Marlene. They are always together, and some beautiful photographs have been taken of them with their tails wrapped around one another and standing side by side.

Recently Marlene was not too well, and we had to keep her in a cage to run some tests, all the time she was inside with us Narcisco was hanging around outside the door and even once he came inside trying to find her. He could smell her and all he knew was he wanted to be with his true love.

Thankfully she was fine and released and Marlene and Narcisco are once again reunited.

Vesta

At only one-month old Vesta was spotted by a tourist inside a temple in one of Rome's many ancient sites. They were concerned and didn't want to leave him there so called for help from the TA.

Paola as you know from previous stories is a champion at catching cats and through knowing many of the archaeologists she has access to many places we cannot go! Lucky for us and even more lucky for Vesta!

It wasn't easy because Vesta did not want to be caught but Paola would not give up and she succeeded eventually! Vesta was brought to Torre Argentina and given the name Vesta.

Six weeks later after being placed into foster care due to his young age he was brought back to the shelter but unfortunately was just as feral as when he was once found.

Something else which was discovered on his return was that Vesta who everyone though was a female was a male! By now it was too complicated to change his name and so to this day he still goes by the name of Vesta. It suits him well as he is such a big boy and it's a strong name.

Vesta was kept in the nursery for a while in the hope that he might find a home soon however the longer stay resulted in him catching an eye infection and now he is easily recognised for his cloudy right eye which gives him a bit of character and means he stands out from the other black cats!

With no adoption forthcoming he was released from the Nursery but stays nearby, watching from where he chooses! He is always around somewhere but those who want to see him cannot always rely on it for sometimes he can be a bit elusive... and it's become quite a celebration if you are lucky enough to see him!

He is a big chunky friendly boy and some people are even lucky enough to have the honour of rubbing his big tummy. If you do spot Vesta be sure to take a photo fast and share it with the group! We all love Vesta, but we just don't see as much of him as we would like to.

Liutprando

Liutprando is a very large black cat who joined us in September 2016. He is easily recognisable by his LONG legs and lovely white tuft of chest hair!

He is a very sweet boy and Valentina is rather fond of him and would be the first to admit to him being her favourite cat of all!!! We often find them smooching together and giving each other dreamy looks across the room. You can be sure wherever Valentina is Liutprando is never far behind! A real-life love story.

Who can resist him he's so sweet!

When he arrived because he was so young and indeed very sweet and affectionate we thought he would be adopted straight away... and he was he was .... immediately.... and then straight away he was returned. Unfortunately, Liutprando does not like dogs and the family who had just adopted him had one at home.

Therefore, and luckily for us he has remained with us. He did not argue with the other cats and was everyone's friend. He has a sweet tooth and you can be sure wherever there is food or cakes to be found he is first in the queue!

He is a handsome, nice and reserved guy with a big heart and the most beautiful long legs you could dream of!!!

Obelix

Obelix arrived in Torre Argentina in January 2017 when he was already a "middle-aged" man who sadly had spent the first part of his life on a terrace.

Poor Obelix, so sad for him but we know that the life he now shares with us here at the TA is a world away from the one he once knew!

He was not sterilized when he arrived and in precarious physical condition, which sadly got worse upon arrival at the shelter, probably the change in adapting to a new environment.

We did everything we could to help him recover and thankfully with time and hard work we can say that we finally succeeded because after a whole year Obelix is now not only a beautiful cat but a healthy cat!!

Obelix is free to live where he chooses and very often comes to keep us company because he loves humans so much! He is a larger boy but a very sweet and friendly boy. You can easily find him around the office area in one of the beds, often choosing to steal Disturbia's bed and squeezing his large body into it!

He also enjoys lying around on the many cat trees observing the room! He enjoys time in the nursery as well as the office, he doesn't love the other cats however as much as us humans but fortunately for everyone he is a gentle giant and never argues ... he does like to hang out with his twin friend Paoletto to confuse us as to who is who... both share the same black and white markings and little cute black moustache lips!!!!

Obelix deserves a wonderful happy life after his past years which were sad lonely and miserable, and we will do what we can for him to make him happy every day.

Zanzara

Beautiful Zanzara was one of the four kittens who were abandoned at the Ufficio dei Diritti Animali (Office of Animal Rights) and taken to Torre Argentina.

After being rescued and given a chance to find a new home two of the kittens were lucky and found a home but Zanzara and brother Calabrone remained with us.

Calabrone sadly passed away in 2015. Leaving with us now only sweet Zanzara. Although beautiful tabbies can sometimes become lost in a crowd, Zanzara, now an older lady is generally quite friendly, so she really stands out!

With her beautiful coat and markings, she really is unique in her own right! However, she can be sometimes be unpredictably moody and she will let you know when she has had enough loving or when she wants to have some space or quiet time.

She chooses to spend most of her time in the main room of the shelter in the beds and enjoys the caresses of the visitors and meeting everyone. She is the perfect cat to visit as you can be sure she will always be around to greet you.

We hope that Zanzara enjoys her peaceful life at the shelter and she certainly never complains and seems happy to be here with us. Let's hear it for Zanzara!

Giotto

Giotto is an old cat who moved into the shelter in October of 2017. His age is unknown exactly, but we think he may be around ten years old.

To decide his name, we created a fun survey on our Facebook group and the winning name was Giotto after the famous painter. Just think he could have been named Elvis if more people than Silvia Z had voted for that choice! Giotto was the clear winner and we certainly think he suits his masculine and wonderful name.

Giotto is a super friendly cat and coming from a colony it's no surprise that he is FIV positive. Giotto also suffered from bilateral entropion, which is a genetic condition where both eye lids turn inward causing a lot of pain from the eyelashes rubbing and many possible infections. If left too long untreated the result can often be blindness. Giotto has had to go through two surgeries to fix this problem and save his eye sight. The first operation wasn't as successful as we had hoped however the second one worked.

He isn't fully blind and although his sight is damaged a little he can still see to some degree. We were very happy with how his wounds healed and his progress. This condition can also return so Giotto will now stay with us so that we can continue to give him the best care if he needs it at any time in the future.

He lives happily in the nursery where he is doing great. More than happy just to let someone pamper him! He loves to spend his days sitting on the knees of visitors and beware, if you bend down close to where he is sitting he is so fast to jump onto your back and shoulders. He sits like a little mountain lion. With his beautiful orange coat, he certainly looks the part.

He has the cutest little voice and sounds like the little old man he is. A little old roar from a lion. His face is full of character and we wish he could speak to tell us his story, so we can fill in all the blanks of his life that we just don't know and cannot know.

He was recently diagnosed with kidney failure on top of all his other problems and for this we feel very sad. He started the same treatments which have worked so well for Smemorina and we hope he can have a longish life with us here.

He certainly loves his life very much. Recently he has enjoyed being carried around in the arms of visitors like a baby snuggling his little head into their necks. He is so full of love that everyone who visits and meets sweet Giotto falls deeply in love with him.

It seems he has a magic spell that he puts on everyone and he makes sure we will always think of him with a heart full of love and affection.

Our dear sweet old gentle Giotto.

Delacroix

In times of loss we also find new life and new hope! Our new little friend ready to be loved comes in the form of our newest addition to the nursery.

The sweet, shy, adorable, beautiful Delacroix.

Delacroix arrived to us from a little place near the sea but not too far from Rome. A town called Pomezia.

Here we work with another shelter and a little cat was brought into their care as part of the trap neuter return programme. Federica from the shelter felt that Delacroix was not a candidate for return due to his condition.

Delacroix at only 2 years of age was suffering from a viral rhinotracheitis where he had an aggressive form of feline herpes which is common in colonies of cats. Both his eyes needed to be removed and he was already completely blind just like our Ray-Charles.

He also tested positive for FIV which we deal with everyday so for us it was not a problem and honestly receiving Delacroix was a gift. Another new life to welcome to our safe place and love!

He has only recently been allowed to join the main nursery after his operations and has taken a little bit of time to settle in. He is very shy, but he is always purring. Such a sweet boy we know he is going to be very popular with everyone who meets him.

He will settle in soon and get used to the other cats and nursery life and so if you are coming to visit make sure you look out for this adorable little guy! He deserves a lot of love

Disturbia

In April 2015 an old lady sadly passed away leaving behind her cat and dog. The orphaned animals were left alone for about a month, cat inside and dog outside.

Rumours were the lady's family intended to "dispose" of the animals and so were taken seriously. A neighbour had keys to the house to feed the cat but didn't have permission to enter. Aware of the reputation of the family he was not comfortable going inside, only feeding the cat when safe to do so.

The dog, outside, was taken in by another relative. Word got out about the cat's situation and a volunteer at a shelter acted to get the cat out of the house.

The volunteer had her spayed and vaccinated. Yet despite this care and kindness it was a shock to find out that the cat was anything but grateful!!!

At first it looked as if she was easy to handle, but once in the volunteer's home, she became aggressive and unmanageable to the point where the volunteer could no longer keep her and begged us to take the cat in. In the shelter the cat still did not behave any better which is why she was named "Disturbia", an invented name but quite accurate to describe the cat's disturbing and easily disturbed character.

When Disturbia was settled she could be free, immediately she stormed out of her cage, but it was a surprise that she did not take off for the Area Sacred. Instead, she found her basic needs consisting of a litter box and a chair in a corner in front of the Transit Room where we provide temporary care for colony cats.

When we improved her abode by also providing a personal mini cat apartment Disturbia had found happiness at last.

Her manners have gradually improved; now she comes inside to look for strokes and even likes being picked up and to be held in somebody's lap, but she still turns into a feline Mr. Hyde without warning or reason!

She is obviously still "disturbed" and will find it hard to find a home.

Now we are lucky to have endless photos of her lying in the strangest positions with her tummy out for the world to see... this girl can sleep anywhere and anytime! She's a firm favourite with visitors and indeed the volunteers! Mellowing as she becomes older and the years pass by Disturbia is quite the character and a firm favourite with all who meet her.

Gasperino

Gasperino was little more than a kitten in June 2015 when he was brought to the shelter from the great Verano cat colony.

Poor Gasperino had been hit by a car and the accident had left him limping on his rear hind leg. Although he had trauma because of the accident he was still very sweet, and we felt a great candidate for a real adoption.

Unfortunately, a full health check-up revealed that he is FIV positive like many feral cats living in colonies.

When he was fully healed and free to choose where he wanted to stay he quickly left the nursery and he discovered new adventures in the Sacred Area. He did not show himself back in the shelter or nursery area for many months!

Now he goes back and forth between the Sacred Area and the shelter depending on how he feels!!!

He loves to be pampered and is very affectionate and he climbs up on everyone ... not easy for small people when he is a big giant! He has become quite enormous! We are lucky he is a giant of the gentle kind and only wants to shower his victims with love and kisses.

Maybe Gasperino hopes that someone will finally open their home to him and we guess he won't stop trying to catch that someone's eye, until then we are happy to have him stay here with us, but we too never give up hope.

Tributes to the ones
we have lost but not
forgotten

Chestnut's Tribute

A Sweet Chestnut
But it was not always so
Abandoned with your siblings as a baby you were the only one not to
find a home
Mellowing through the years you finally became comfortable and
begun to enjoy life
It took a while
But it was worth the time and patience

The chestnut tree symbolises honesty
Chestnut you were very honest
Telling us when you wanted to be loved
And telling us when you wanted to be alone
We always knew where we stood with you
A true cat

You started off life in the most perfect way
A foster of our very own Daniele
And in-fact you became one of his favourite cats
Only recently he spoke of you
One of his favourites he said
Every day he looked for you because you knew to come and take
your medicine

A special bond between you both
Perhaps you did remember how he helped you
All those years ago
That you once shared "his home"
Before he brought you to the nursery
And then he shared "your home"

Sometimes the love found in a cat is not all about kisses
Belly rubs
Head bumps
Sometimes the love is deeper

It is about space and respect
And knowing when love is needed as much as when to be avoided

It is true you mellowed with age and became softer
But we also respected your free will
Your spirit and your kind heart

We will miss you Chestnut
Of course not as much as Daniele
It cannot be possible
And today our heart goes to him
We too experience loss
We know how it feels
And so for him it must be so much greater

Thank you, Chestnut,
For providing to Daniele
A lifelong friend
A steady companion
A bond that no space or time can break

We love you
Fly high and stay sweet
Our little sweet chestnut

So sorry to all the volunteers for the loss of little Chestnut

May she be free and at peace

Until we are together again we will always remember her

Gioella's Tribute

The little blind girl who could see with her heart
How is it possible? many might ask
We may never know or understand
But isn't that a beautiful "thing"?
After all isn't love a feeling?
Isn't it a "thing"?
A sense
We don't need to see love to know it is there
Gioella knew, yes, she knew
She didn't need to see it, she could feel it all around her
This "thing"
This love

We were only gifted with the presence of Gioella towards the last
stages of her life
Because she somehow managed to survive all that time on the
streets
before we were graced with her
This little blind girl, who had suffered in ways we can't and don't
even know how to imagine
An untold secret known only to her
But, you know, there is one thing which touches the heart more than
any other
The ability to love
No matter what Gioella had suffered before we met her
Before we knew her, before we could love her
Despite any cruelty or hardship she had faced
She still had trust
She carried with her in her tiny little heart the ability to trust
To trust the volunteers
To trust each and every visitor
To trust the other cats
Trust allowed her to find comfort in the arms of strangers
She had no fear
No worry that anyone would ever hurt her again

She had no badness in her heart
She was created only of everything that is good in the world
She gave us hope
Encouragement that in dark days there will always be brighter days
to follow
To open up our hearts
For if we do, we may just experience the greatest thing of all
This "thing"
This love

So, we thank you, Gioella
For yet again, through you, this tiny little being
This tiny little blind girl
With a tiny little heart
Yet, with the biggest heart of all
We learnt again a lesson to help us in life
We learn from those who cannot speak
And those who cannot see
But those who can feel

Never be afraid
Never give up
Never close your heart
For always there is sunshine in life if you allow there to be

I wish you full recovery now
To be complete and whole again
To have the warm sunshine in your eyes
Perfect vision
To see the world in colour
So bright and beautiful
Like the colours of your heart
May you sleep well our angel friend

Our little blind girl
blind, but with the sight which is more special than any other
We love you always Gioella
Our sweet Gioella

And when you close your eyes you can be sure our arms are
wrapped around you
Like a blanket
A blanket of love that you used to adore so much
We will never let you go
Rest well
In our love you are never alone
You are in our arms exactly where you loved to be

Ray-Charles's Tribute

When we write about the ones we love the words can often flow
After all to write with love comes from the heart
But what happens when that heart is broken?

Ray-Charles you have left us now
Our hearts have shattered into a million pieces
today we are here with only tears and sadness

We are thankful for you
We knew what a true love was
We are grateful for all the smiles you gave to us every day
But we are empty
A part of us left with you

Yesterday I read the most beautiful thing
" I saw the angel in the marble and I carved until I set him free"

You were the certainly the angel in the marble
Maybe you were ready to go?
You sent a sign for us to remember you
Perhaps you wanted to be in control of your own tribute
To put your own stamp upon it
For this could only be a beautiful reflection of you

 You trusted us
slowly you became confident
making the nursery your home
You loved that place
Jumping all over the beds
Our little ninja boy
Blind but with the sight from within
to understand
to share
to love
to grow

and to be known

Everyone who met you felt love
they felt admiration at watching you
they felt inspired to know that beyond any impairment or difficulties
there is always hope
and there can always be good times

What a joy for you Ray-Charles
This little being
full of fun and sweetness
You were all good
You were perfect to us
Our little blind ninja

You leave us now but only from sight
Because we hold you forever close to us
Deep in our hearts
Another angel in heaven
At the side of the rainbow bridge
With your friends
Waiting for us
So we can all be together once again

Be happy dear Ray-Charles
Be free
Know we love you and the loss of you is severe
The pain is beyond words
We cannot find these words

We are sorry we could not do more
You passed with love
You lived in love
You will remain in love

Our little warrior never forgotten
Our beautiful boy
Our Ray-Charles

Posiedone's Tribute

The words we never wish we ever had to write yet here we are writing this tribute to you. Where can one start when we think of you sweet boy? So much to say but we could spend forever talking about you. Why not? when talking about you brings us joy and happiness and puts a smile on our faces

You were given the name Posiedone because you came from a town near the sea. Completely blind and you had cancer in your ears. We cared for you and made you better in any way we could. You had found a new life with us and quickly settled in.

Little-big Posiedone, blind, no ears and no teeth yet to us you were the most beautiful boy in the world. We did not see anything other than love on your face and hope in your eyes and you loved your new life.

You loved it so much you wanted to be everywhere and be with everyone making friends with the other cats and every visitor who came to visit fell in love. You didn't let your blindness stop you and you tried to be the same as everyone else. You were no ninja like Ray-Charles though! Even though you maybe thought you were!

Your adventurous nature caused you to fall one time and you hurt yourself badly. Silvia Z always called you dumb (in an affectionate way) but we know you just wanted to be the same as all the others. You spent quite a lot of time afterwards in a cage to heal and yet you did not complain. You let the time pass by being polite as always and content. Who taught you these beautiful manners? Who had loved you once before? You were already neutered so we know you once had a home. The rest we cannot and will never know. Maybe we don't need to know. We just accept you arrived, and you stayed.

So now you were also limping, somewhat adding to your charm and yet still you were elegant, in your own Posiedone way! You were all the things you were never meant to be, yet you were!

You were those things Posiedone and we loved you for it! So gentle and so sweet and you became a heart throb! The cat we all adored from all over the world. What was it about you? One does not need to even know.

All we need to know is that you were, and you are, and you will always be.

The nursery is missing you. People are missing you. Writing this I am missing you even though I never met you. You have left a hole and your lack of presence is noticeable. Our hearts are aching for the volunteers who cared for you so well. For the visitors who never got to meet you because of your untimely passing. For the distance adopters who made you, their son, and loved you as if you were their family and in their own home.

That gap will be filled by another no doubt. It always happens. It's a life cycle. The circle of life as they say.

You arrived on 11th August 2017 the day Gianburrasca passed over to the rainbow bridge. For that we thank you. You taught us it is ok to love another. It is ok to find a space in our hearts. You healed us from the incredible pain we suffered, and you gave us hope again. You taught us to fall in love. The love for you was so strong but more than that it was real.

So, we will love again, to honour you Posiedone. We will never stop loving you, but we will do what you taught us. We will also be grateful for the short time you were in our lives.

I truly believe every cat is sent to us at a time and for a reason. Your reason was love. If love is your legacy, then Posiedone be proud for you have filled the world of love yet again. What a beautiful thing.

A blind cat, you didn't need your eyes to love.

You just did.

It is a feeling after all.

Thank you Posiedone for sharing your life with us. We are going to miss you more than you can ever know. Your memory will always live on. We will make sure of that. Today we honour you. Your beauty, your soul, your heart and your memory.

I never met you, but I knew you
I never met you, but I love you
I never met you, but I won't ever forget you

Sleep well with the angels Posiedone, now you have your wings. Fly high and watch over us. I hope your friends welcome you and give you the love you so craved, received and gave here on earth.

Faberge's Tribute

A happy tribute for our golden boy Faberge like the golden egg.

Elegant and majestic, a treasure to behold. This is what you were and always will be.

With your fiery red ember coat shining where ever you lay in the warm Roman sun.

This is how we will remember you.

With your nose up in the air, always smelling everything around you, you were the king in your castle.

You came in a bad way with your crooked jaw, but it made you even more majestic and unique just like every Faberge egg that was ever produced. A treasure so sacred and to be cherished. Our Faberge.

Oh, how you loved to stay outdoors, lying on the walls, always with your nose pointing to the sky, almost like you were looking up because really you were looking down upon everyone around you.

Maybe you knew and understood your name and what it meant? Maybe you knew you were majestic and beautiful, and you were a special one?

Maybe we were just your humble servants.

Those who knew you loved you very much and today there are a lot of broken hearts.

How you loved to eat, and this was the one time you were just a "normal boy" with no majestic table manners in sight! You gobbled up the food you loved so much, and you did not take much care in how you ate and often you ended up wearing the food all over your face because your crooked jaw made it.... well ... just not so easy to eat in a dignified and royal manner but you didn't care, it didn't make your appetite any less!

And we didn't care either! In fact, it became you. It is how we often captured you in photographs. It made us smile inside and outside. We were just so delighted to see you eating after many years of hardship on the streets and knowing you didn't have to worry where your next meal was coming from!

When we didn't "suit you" anymore and you were bored of us you decided that you wanted a "change of scenery" and moved to the shoe shop across the street! How funny! Roberta greeted you and welcomed you there! We were told shoe sales increased because of your presence! And all the cats at TA adore shoes but no one was so bold to make the leap of faith except you!

You did however come back to us when you weren't so well. You trusted us to be there for you and to do the right thing. And we did. But how it was hard to make that decision. A month already filled with grief and we then also must lose our golden boy, our red ember Faberge, with his fiery coat and huge personality.

We know it was right and we know you would have approved otherwise you would not have come back to us. We will never forget you Faberge. Please look after us as you join your other friends.

I hope it's happy where you are at the rainbow bridge and you are smelling the air around you. Remember to eat well but always eat messy! This is you and do not change for anyone.

We shall miss seeing you in "your place" and Roberta sends you her love also.

We think of you now with a smile on our face for in a world that is often black and white your love was like a rainbow, colourful and beautiful.

Sleep well old boy. And how we will miss you! You will live on in the warmth of the Roman sun and we will feel you with us always that's for sure.

Amanita's Tribute

An exotic name, beautiful from the tongue
Yet it means a little poisonous mushroom
How funny to be a little poisonous mushroom yet to us you are just a
little mushroom

A special little mushroom
A beautiful mushroom
Amanita the mushroom

Amanita you are our mushroom

You were part of a collection, one of many,
a collection of cats living in terrible conditions
I have no doubt the lady who kept you felt she was doing the best
She most certainly loved you in her own way
But, with her collection of cats came tragedy
A sad life for you
and lack of care led to you losing your sight
But finally you were safe with us
You, your sister Bubbala
and your brother Champignon

You all arrived together,
quickly Bubbala found her golden basket,
her forever home
Champignon waits all the time for his
meanwhile having fun
and becoming fat with his chicken parties

You were never destined to find a home,
with poorly health you were to gain a lifelong home with us
We just didn't know it would be so short

Here you arrived and straight away
became a restoration project
To repair and resolve, to mend and heal
To care and love unconditionally

Yet sadly it was never going to be enough to save you, Our dear Amanita

We are so sorry

When life brings us rainbows sometimes it also is followed by a dark cloud
We wish to blow away the dark cloud with love
But sometimes the love just is not enough, and the clouds stay and they cover our rainbow

Amanita, how very sad for you that at this time you finally found the best people
The ones who would care for you
Who would hold you
Feed you
Clean you
And most of all love you
And all of that was snatched away in a heartbeat
With this cruel disease
We tried to save you but we cannot allow any of our precious jewels to suffer
And certainly not our special mushroom

Amanita your time with us was short but we hope we brought some light into your dark life
You certainly filled us with light but most of all joy and love
We hope that you knew what it was to feel gentle hands caress you
We hope that you enjoyed the taste of good food
The feeling of a warm, soft bed
The brushes on your fur with tender hands
The soft voices who spoke to you
The ones who whispered into your ear the words you deserved to hear
"Amanita I love you"

We will miss you and we are sorry we could not do more
Thank you for trusting in us to do what is right for you
We did the kindest thing for you
We tried to save you
And know what we did was with love in our hearts
Even if it meant our hearts were left broken in two

We will rebuild again and think of you with strength
We will think of you with courage
Our strong girl
Who never gave up
We will never forget you Amanita
And we will make sure we care for Champignon,
for you, as we know you would want us to

You will live on in love
Our little poisonous mushroom
Our mushroom
Our precious gift
Our Amanita

The most beautiful mushroom, you are now with your friends at the
rainbow bridge
Blow away that darkness Amanita and shower us with colour and
light
Our rainbow in the sky
Our Amanita

Marzapane's Tribute

A sweet name for a sweet boy
You lived your life to the fullest, you loved life, it can truly be said,
for you showed us in every way just how much

You adored playing, eating and being with people as much as being
with your friends
You loved everyone, a heart as big as the ocean with enough love for
the whole world

The leader of the pack
The popular one
The one who was everyone's friend and who's friend everyone
wanted to be
A real "guy" yet still a sweet boy, very much loved and adored
worldwide

You made us laugh with your antics, your games and your fun
But you made us cry, those of us who could not meet you in time for
we learned in shock of your passing
So sudden, so unexpected but how can this news ever be expected
with one so full of life and vitality?

So many questions we have and of which we shall never know the
answers
So for this we shall not seek the answers and simply rejoice in the
knowledge and understanding that you loved your life

You left us a gift
You left us with a reminder that life is short
We should be happy, we should have fun
We should eat and be merry
We should love our friends
We should embrace our chubbiness and smile at it for we know you
always stole the hearts of the ladies even if you did carry some extra
pounds
We should smile and enjoy what we have, the little things in life

Do in our lives what you did in yours
Smile and love, it's quite simple
This is for you Marzapane
Today we cried, we cannot lie
We shall miss you greatly, but we shall remember you
We shall smile the way you did, we shall laugh at the memories of you
We shall enjoy the happiness you bestowed upon us
We shall love you forever
Thank you for your gift Marzapane

We are sorry your time with us was short, but we are happy to know you loved it
You were a blessing to us, you enriched our lives if only for a short time, how many in life can say this?
You were a treasure, a joy
We love you with all of us, a love like you, so pure and true
Sleep with the angels now my boy, with your beloved friends and shine upon us with the others we lost and love so much

We shall remember you
Rainbows are our friends

Sweet Marzapane – you are simply the icing on the cake

Cocoon's Tribute

Dearest Cocoon, I didn't quite know what to write to you and for you that would be fitting enough to be "your tribute" sweet boy

However, I thought about you and I remembered some of the wonderful things people told me about you. I thought of what you meant to the people who knew you. The ones who talked to me about you.

There were so many questions unanswered. Who were you? Where did you come from? Did you suffer before? Was your life before you came here difficult?

You arrived as an old man, who had been through things we cannot imagine, and we don't want to imagine but for you it was real, it was your life.

You were only here for a short time but oh, how you loved in that short time. Making up for a life on the streets, unloved, unwanted and uncared for.

You LOVED in a way only you could. You loved pure, and strong and hard.

You loved with your whole being, even though you yourself were so small and fragile.

I was told all you wanted was to LOVE. To find comfort and a warm place. You would stay there happily for hours just purring and expressing your happiness and your joy at something so simple, to be held.

In some ways your name suited you, cocoon, you were cocooned in love and it became your happy place.

You were welcomed here, to be part of the family and do you know how many people adored you? How many people noticed you? Who wanted to see you again, who asked about you? Those people won't ever forget you.

So, my dear sweet boy, our little cocoon you will always be remembered.

I know one lady who spent a week with you. She never stopped talking about you. You weren't the one she was excited to meet for the first time yet in your quiet and gentle unassuming way you became the lime light, the star, the sole focus and everything you deserved to be. You found your own way to "shine".

So, cocoon you made it, from the hard times on the street to the place which we on earth call "cat heaven" you reached the top! And you were shown love in your final days, I know all about your heat pad, the cuddles and caresses and how you still loved to eat. I was told quite simply you were not ready, and you did not want to die.

You would tell us when you were ready.

That lady left you, she knew you did not have long, she gave you the heat pad, she gave you a blanket and she kissed your head as she said goodbye. She worried about you, she asked about you, and just almost 2 days later you "chose" to go.

In your own time and on your terms, when YOU were ready.

Perhaps you had already found your one true love? Maybe it was a short love, but it was the best love? Maybe it was the strongest love and it couldn't get any better than that?

I like to think that you drifted off to sleep and were dreaming. I hope you were dreaming of everything you came to know that was beautiful and wonderful. I hope you were on a warm knee in the dream being held, in a cocoon just like your name.

Sleep well my dear old boy, we did not have you for a long time, but we had you for the best and most important time.

Until we meet again fly high above the rainbows during the day time and shine upon us in the evening, be our guide and our comfort as we were to you. Thank you for the memories Cocoon. You will be forever loved.

Sonora's Tribute

A melody
A song
A little old lady who lived quietly
A peaceful girl

To many you blended into the background
Nothing to make you stand out from the others
Simply black with a little white chest
But the most magnificent white whiskers one could ever wish to see
Beautiful in your own unassuming way
So you see you did stand out to those who cared enough to look at
you

Happy to spend days lazing and sleeping
Enjoying the parties and having your fair share
One of the sweetest old ladies we ever had the pleasure of knowing
So many fell in love with your sweetness
You loved to hug and stay in the arms of those who took the time to
caress you
Sitting on knees
Always coming forward to offer yourself to us
Purring with joy
Always calm and joyful
Perhaps you were a healer
Reaching out to those who needed you most
An important job we think!

How sorry we are when these pleasures must end
For the time comes when we see things
We notice things
We see you are already old but become older
You don't move so well
Or eat so much
You sleep more and more
And wish to be alone

The purr is still there
You are present but something inside you told us enough
You were ready

How sad we are for you to depart
To leave us here
To be gone from sight
To gain those angel wings we all know are so beautiful
To take you high above
Up to that rainbow bridge where so many have gone before
And we know so many will also come to join you

Sonora you were sweet in life
And will remain sweet in your passing
We know you have important things to do now
You have souls to heal
Someone must need you more than we do here
Perhaps a friend called to you
They missed you
You were their strength

So we go on but we will be thankful every day
For the life of you
For the love you were so generous to share with us
This little old lady
Our sweet girl
Unselfish to the end
Giving all of you to us so generously
We thank you Sonora
Now go get those golden wings
For you will wear them beautifully
Just like your magnificent white whiskers

Zebra's Tribute

Only in some lifetimes are we graced with a cat who stays with us for such a long time that they can celebrate a 14th birthday

Zebra is one of those and for us we are grateful and happy to have had so many years of joy

With three failed adoptions it seemed that Zebra was destined to share a life with us here at TA. Only this summer she had her 14th birthday celebrations which we shared with everyone and she was happy to share her cake with her friend Fabula

A cat with diabetic problems she loved to eat, a lot!! Sharing always the lunches of the volunteers and with a good palette she sought out the finer things in life, spaghetti as a real Italian cat and falafels too which she would happily nibble on. We were just happy to see her eat with gusto. With her diabetic problems she was not allowed a lot of these treats but when she did receive them she really enjoyed them a lot

However, with old age comes bad health and deterioration and lately Zebra became very thin and did not wish to eat so much. For us this weight loss and certainly loss of appetite was Zebra's own way of speaking to us.

Cats will always let us know when "it is time" and over the past few days we think she was trying to find a way to leave the nursery to go off and to die alone as cats so often do

We did not want this lonely ending for our sweet Zebra and so the vet was called to give her the most calm and beautiful passing over to the rainbow bridge. In Monica's arms and purring to the end, she was happy to be set free and join her many friends who we know were waiting for her

Lets celebrate the life of our sweet Zebra for she was one of our oldest long-term residents and we know that she loved her life here. Happy to spend many days lying upon the merchandise in full view of the visitors. Often, she preferred to stay behind the scenes too working with us in the office

Really, we cannot wish for any more than one of our cats to have a long life, Zebra achieved this

We always wish for them not to have suffered a life on the streets and Zebra achieved this too

In-fact she had a great life, full of care, good food, company from humans and other cat friends, visitors and always with the comfort of bedding, blankets and her very own personalised bed too thanks to Valentina!

We were lucky Zebra did not come to us from the streets so never suffered what many of our cats have yet she was always grateful, and we believe she knew

A real graceful, kind girl

We think maybe Zebra was blessed but indeed we were the ones who were blessed to know her and have her for such a long time. We are grateful

The greatest gift in life is to be loved, a real endless love and Zebra you had this

We know you are happy now. You are at peace just how you wanted, and you know you were loved and always will be loved

We shall remember you Zebra and when we do we will smile. Thank you for the memories. We hope you have lots of spaghetti and falafels at the rainbow bridge beside you in your golden basket. May you dance on moonbeams and fly high with love sent to heaven from all of us below

We will miss you

Gottardo's Tribute

There are some cats who's passing hits you like a thunderbolt and truly shocks you to the core. It's a passing you know is inevitable yet in your own way you hope the day will never come

Gottardo you have left us so suddenly and we were not ready. How could we ever have been ready?

Living every day knowing you were with us was a joy itself! We were the lucky ones! To see you wearing your beautiful scarves like the gentleman you were. A beautiful boy inside and out! Strong and independent you loved your life at Torre Argentina and you loved people

Always lazing outside in the warm sunshine under or in the flowerpots and on the tables in the office you made sure everyone saw you and you became a real poser boy! You were easily recognisable except when you were mistaken for Rubio your "almost" twin brother!

Everyone adored you so much. Especially dear Raptus who now faces another tragic love story and we shall have to work hard to mend yet again her little broken heart

You had fans everywhere, the famous "Gottardo" or affectionately you were also known as "Gotty" by Silvia Z who often called you this! and you especially touched the heart of our dearest volunteers. One could say you were and are one of their favourites. They would admit to having a soft spot for you filled with love and adoration.

My heart is breaking for them as well as all the parents who distance adopted you and who care for and love you so much. Such a shock is felt at your sudden passing and there will be a river of tears flowing for you today.

Your name means "Strong" and this is indeed exactly what you were right to the end! Defying all odds to recover from serious injuries from a car accident leaving you in a bad way. You fought and even your eyesight which we thought you lost returned

You were not a young boy and for this we are grateful. To know you had many happy years with us brings us lasting happiness. We know you loved your life here and we loved having you! If only everything could last forever

You disappeared for one day and maybe you knew you were going to die and maybe you wished to spare us the pain, but you did the right thing and you were brave enough to come back to us. You allowed us to try and help you, but it was just so fast and there was nothing we could do. For this we are sorry Gottardo, but we were with you to the very end

We will be with you forever now as we remember you with love and happiness! Thank you, sweet Gottardo, for the friendship you shared, for the laughs you gave us when you had heatstroke because you didn't know to stay out of the sun, the laughs at hiding from Raptus behind the cat-door and the smiles at the memories of you wearing your smart clothes looking deliciously handsome

Monica told us "you are in paradise now" an extension then it is from the paradise you once knew here to the one up above at the rainbow bridge where all your friends will be waiting to greet you. Sleep well angel Gottardo, we are so sorry you have gained your wings, but we know in heaven there is a place for you. Until we meet again look down upon us and when we see a bright star in the sky we shall know it is you smiling and that you are happy once again! We hope you are wearing a nice scarf!

Stay beautiful our forever precious Gottardo, we will love you always.

Lumachina's Tribute

Lumachina we loved you from the moment we first saw you. With your beautiful little mermaid tail people came to notice you and you captured our hearts. You looked like you had no hope or chance in life with the condition you were in and yet you found your own way to make it through each day and to survive. It was so hard even at Torre Argentina for you in the beginning so how you managed all those months outside we cannot even imagine

The length of time you were left this way caused considerable damage to you and for this you have sadly paid the price. It pains me to know that someone who did this to you carries on living, unaware. Not seeing the repercussions of their actions or to look into your innocent and beautiful eyes to know that even through your hurt and trauma still were able to show love and kindness

Battling against everything Lumachina, YOU, this little girl, came to us and even though you were only here for a short time you still left us with a paw print on our hearts

To write this is heart breaking but though the tears and sadness I am still glad

I am glad for the life of you
I am glad for knowing you
I am glad for the determination and strength you have shown us

A strength not even some humans can show. I am glad that you found your way to us so that we could show you what it was to be loved

To be cared for
To be comfortable
To be happy
To be you

Even though your time with us was short I like to think you had a taste of the good life. You climbed the beds. You ate at the fish parties. You even had your own spa day

You allowed people to show you the love you truly deserved and for that we can only be grateful. We appreciate you Lumachina. We love you and we must learn from you

Every day you showed more and more ability to adapt and conquer everything around you and this is remarkable. You were remarkable. You were strong, and you never gave up. Although you are now gone from us please know Lumachina that you are still very much loved

It could have been easy not to love you, not to see you, but why do that? To spare ourselves? When you did nothing wrong. Why deny you that small time on earth to be appreciated and known and loved

So, instead we celebrate you

We all looked at you and yes, we felt terrible sadness for the condition you were in, but we also felt amazing pride that you fought all odds. When everything was stacked against you, it was your time to shine and you shone! Like the brightest star in the sky you shone. You made us feel hope that even in a bad situation there is always a way to find love, to feel love and to know love

You became Love

Life is often cruel, and we always say that these passing's leave us a little more broken but also our hearts overflow, because we again know what it is to feel love. A real deep true never-ending love

It is so cruel Lumachina that when you did find your happiness it was so short, but we are happy that you came to us and did not pass somewhere alone on the street. It is certainly a day of sadness because we will miss you so very much

Your life meant something
You meant everything
You will not be forgotten
You are Lumachina
You will always be Lumachina
You are our beautiful amazing little mermaid snail

Onice's Tribute

If you check the meaning of this name it means a beautiful chalcedony. When you work with the energy of the chalcedony you will feel more positivity in your heart, your mind and your soul. What happens when that Onice or chalcedony must leave us....? Well, we are left... still... with the lingering feeling of positivity in our hearts and our minds and our soul

Like a precious gem, forever set in the stone it is made from, Onice was and is just that, a precious gem. We are sorry you had to leave us, but we understand that here at TA, sadly nothing is forever. Except, like you, a precious gem who lives on in our memories

A free life is what you chose to live, the warm Roman sun always shining on you. Your black onyx coat often turning a warm burn amber. Again, like a precious gem stone changing with the light. Your elegance was bestowed upon us

One friend I know, who loved you very much, called you "art" and described you as "a poem". In your own way you truly were. She saw this in you because in her own way she loved you and I know always will. She was deeply saddened by your passing and we were too

One of our Area Sacred residents often overlooked because you did not have special needs, you were not in the office or the nursery and you were not always in full view. You didn't often appear in photographs by us or by other visitors

You just lived

A quiet unassuming life, still there, but only to those who chose to see you. You never had to be a favourite or be known to everyone. Yet we can still miss you for what you are and what you were, and we can still, while looking at you, admire the simplicity of your life

The simplicity of your beauty yet the complexity of just how beautiful you were and still are. In so many ways exactly like a chalcedony, made of different strands, woven together. A gentle and unassuming soul

We still see you Onice, when we close our eyes, sitting on the stairs, next to the balustrade looking up at us. Gentle kind eyes who saw into our souls, a warm and tender love and who we look at with a warm and tender love

For those of us who knew you we truly are blessed. For those of us who did not see you we ask you to next time look a little harder, look for the ones who go un-noticed for among those you will certainly find your own chalcedony, a treasure, a gem and perhaps another special one like Onice

Fly high our loved one, we thank you for your presence and the love you shared with us. It was our pleasure to know you. We know you are now a bright star in the sky. We miss you and we think of you with a heart full of love. Send us another rainbow please in the warm amber colours of you

Lalique's Tribute

Some very sad news at TA today. Unfortunately, we had to say goodbye to our beautiful and young baby Lalique who was sadly hit and killed by a car last night / early morning

We do not know what happened, but we know how upsetting this is and it is such a horrid thing to happen. It's bad enough when our babies are poorly and ill but when this happens at the hands of humans driving cars it makes it so much harder. Such a young life and so much life to live

We wonder and try to think of ways of how we can avoid this, but we cannot. Some cats are happy to stay indoors or avoid the roads, some are mischievous and wander far. Was she attracted by a human, was she chasing a bird, or was it normal for her to cross the road.... so many questions we cannot answer

We are all deeply saddened at TA by this as she was recovering from recent surgery on her teeth and we hoped that with a full recovery she could live a long and happy life with us. Along with her brother Lladro who is sadly left on his own now

Such a sweet and playful girl certainly with a mind of her own she will be missed by all of us here and we are sorry. This is not a nice situation and we hope she did not suffer

Please say a little prayer for our baby girl Lalique and may her sweet soul rest in peace as she goes off to the rainbow bridge to join many of her friends who have also passed, and may she look down on us as we look up to our new bright shining star in heaven

We love you Lalique

Tina's Tribute

Sometimes we are graced with cats who have a special presence. Ones who despite what has happened to them just have a love for life and continue to fight despite all odds

Well, here today, we sadly said goodbye to one of those cats. Our special girl Tina has sadly passed over to the rainbow bridge to be with her friends

She had suffered trouble after trouble not even considering the condition she arrived to us in

We saved her, and she fought!

Even recently when she had another health scare, again she fought

Through everything she never lost a sense of herself. A real happy chatterbox who liked to talk and talk and talk and talk!

This petite tiny little black beauty lived life to the fullest being adored here at TA. Often unseen but no less special to us she stole the hearts of many and was and continues to be so very loved! We were so very lucky to be graced with her presence and we will miss her very much

We know she is now free for suffering and this means everything to us. As much as we wish to hold onto our loves forever sometimes we know that this is not always right, and we do what we must

So, with a pain free and peaceful passing she left us, and she shines now above us, another star shining over TA

Moonbeams in the evening and rainbows in the day

We love you our dear sweet Tina

Thank you for being you!

We were so very lucky to know you and we never gave up on you, just as you never gave up fighting but when it's time it is time and we respect you

Our forever angel, little friend and forever love, our precious Tina

Oniria's Tribute

A friend once described TA as a hospice and for some cats this is true. For one little cat, Oniria, it really was true

A hospice is a place for short term care for cats or people at the end of their life. So, if that's the definition then maybe in some way's TA plays another important role in giving that end of life care in the form of a hospice

Little Oniria came to us only in February so she hasn't been with us very long and already she was a very old lady, no one can be sure of her exact age but more than ten years old. Suffering from health problems from many years surviving on the streets she was thin and bedraggled

However, with her sweet nature she settled into her Nursery life and the relaxed and comfortable environment

We don't have much to say because what can one say in this circumstance, but we can say that every cat no matter how recently they enter the shelter or how long or how young or how old deserves to have their name known and to be given a lovely message or a kiss or a heart or a wish for a smooth journey to the rainbow bridge

You see not all cats are famous Gianburrasca's or Gottardo's but all who enter the shelter are given a name and all leave having a name

Some have long stories and many tales to tell and some just don't have this because maybe they are like Oniria

She just lived quietly but happily and for us this is all that we need to know. She passed away with us and was not alone. She was not hungry, and she was always comfortable and warm while she was here so for that we are thankful!

Even in hard times we look forward because there will always be another cat ready to take her place who needs care and that will happen no matter how long or short it may be

So today we send some love to Oniria as she makes her way over the Rainbow Bridge to join her friends and waits for us to one day be together again

Dadino's Tribute

Our little glamorous tuxedo boy, always dressed to thrill and smart as a button, style your middle name. Ready to paint the town red or dance under the stars like a mini version of Frank Sinatra. Glitz, glamour, elegance and grace is always the air around you.
Your little spindly legs cute and silky with gorgeous white paws like little boots making your tuxedo outfit complete. Your slinky shiny body attracted us all and we fell under your spell

You love to climb and to be where you should not be, an independent mind and we cannot contain this. You were free to live the life that you chose, not the one we forced upon you. A cheeky young boy who loves the outdoors and especially the fresh air

We are sure you are always being naughty somewhere. You don't listen to Monica when she calls for you, defying everyone. A sweet spirit and one we cannot be angry with, you are just too cute

We instead made funny videos of you, your life and your story
You were our very first cat-ur-day cat, our superstar. How wonderful to see these and remember you now, and for always. A moment captured in time, to know you were here and you existed

Dadino you are young, and you lived. You loved your life. Dadino we are going to miss you so much and we hope you will come back to us! We will miss your eyes, irresistible and beautiful
Your face so sweet and so kind. If only we could have known to hold you one last time, to take that final photograph, but we could not know

Now we shall remember you whenever we hear Frank Sinatra sing. We shall imagine you tap dancing on the ruins, with a full orchestra and live band, with spotlights all around you. Dance free in the stars wherever you are

Bless us with your grace for always and eternity, we shall always remember you, our little cloudy eyed boy, we love you Dadino

Agatone's Tribute

We take pride in allowing our cats to be just that. Cats with free spirits and minds of their own!

Although we care for them provide food, shelter and medical care when required many of the "unseen" cats choose to live a solitary life among the ruins of the Area Sacred. Some choose to enjoy a bit of both and one of those such cats is our wonderful Prince Agatone

A gorgeous white cat who arrived with his sister Agathe (who has since been adopted into a home of her own) Agatone remained with us and although he often loved the baskets he also loved being outside too

Part of this risk of course is traffic or indeed people. Now sometimes a cat can just vanish, and we do not know where it goes. It is just never seen again and does not return. Sadly, for us it leaves us with many questions of which we do not have the answers

In the case of our Prince Agatone we have found ourselves in this situation

Our sweet Prince has not returned to us now for 2 months and we have no answers. In a perfect world we hope he found his someone or a home

We do not know

Since we always like to look on the bright side of life we did some detective work...

...we know Agatone is a beautiful cat .... and we know Sir Anthony Hopkins was recently in Rome .... we also know that Sir Anthony loves cats.... and Agatone disappeared around the same time as Anthony Hopkins left Rome after shooting his movie......

In this case it can only be that Sir Anthony stopped by on the way home and fell in love with our Prince Agatone and decided to steal him from us to make him a cat of his own!!!!!

We are very sure that Prince Agatone now lives like a King with his very own golden basket, a crown, a diamond collar, his own private fountain which Smemorina would be envious of, he eats fresh tuna every day and in the morning Sir Tony plays the piano to him to wake him up and in the evening, he plays a soft lullaby to help Agatone sleep

This thought fills us with happiness

Maybe one day Prince Agatone will return but until then we thank you Sir Anthony for taking care of our sweet and beloved Prince

Until we meet again Agatone be happy wherever you are

Happy Gianburrasca Day - The unforgettable Gianburrasca

Some people touch our lives for only an instant
you, my sweet boy, left paw prints on our hearts forever

How can someone so small touch us so greatly? Well you are
Gianburrasca - it is you

You somehow reach the deepest parts of us, the ones who need you
most, showering us with love, a pure and endless love, a love so
strong that it hurts but it is the most beautiful pain because it means
you existed, you were here and you were real and you meant
something to all of us and you are missed so much

Your little face so innocent, always smiling, full of happiness and
filled with love. You never asked for much, you just lived simply.
Happy everyday just to be with people and your friends

You loved life, you loved YOUR life, you loved the nursery, you loved
your friends, especially your best friend Grumpy. You loved to be
close to people, you loved to give love even more than receiving
love. Your heart was big enough for everyone!

Some people could learn a lot from you!
I was lucky, to know you, to have held you, to have looked into your
beautiful eyes, to have seen your beautiful lips smiling up at me

To have felt your warmth, your heart beat and heard your loud
purring, like a motor, fierce and strong. Releasing some of the joy
and happiness you always felt so much

Your heart was surely always overflowing for it will filled with so
much love you just wanted to share with everyone

In life we suffer loss and the pain is incredible,
yet somehow, we find a way to love another
Through doing this we also honour the one we have lost by opening
our hearts once again

It is what you would want, it is what you would ask of us, for cats like you are not selfish, you would be happy for your friends, the ones you knew, and the ones you never had the chance to meet

Our hearts break with your passing but the new love we feel, and share repairs the cracks, and in time we learn to live with the pain. It is true we move on, but we do not ever forget the ones who touched us most

You will always be in our memories
Your name will always be on our lips
You will forever live in our hearts

What was so special about you Gianburrasca? I don't even know, it was just you and you just were. Perhaps we don't need to know. We just need to feel lucky that we lived our life at the same time as you. This is amazing. The size of the whole world and our paths crossed. We lived life at the same time. Somehow and for some reason you ended up at Torre Argentina

Many cats will pass through our lives as we go through this journey called life but there will only ever be one who leaves a mark as strong as you did - Gianburrasca you were my one

I feel so blessed to know you. I will never let your memory die and you shall always be honoured and remembered

I may not see you anymore, but I feel you with me every day. I love you always and today I celebrate the life of you

Happy Gianburrasca Day

You were a gift to the world

My unforgettable Gianburrasca

Thank you

Thank you to each person who has purchased this book and honoured all our cat's past and present.

By doing so you have shown support to the amazing work of the Torre Argentina.

It is impossible to tell the stories of each one as there are so many and the amazing work of Silvia and Lia and the volunteers spans such a long period of time.

Thank you for the life of my dear sweet Gianburrasca without the Torre Argentina our meeting would not have been possible, and I would not have enjoyed knowing him.

Thank you to my husband Jon for believing in me and encouraging me to complete this book. Your support is endless.

Please continue to support this amazing organisation and help save the lives of many more cats, the ones who have not yet reached the shelter and those who no doubt will.

Work like this never ends and we cannot do it without our amazing supporters so to every one of you we thank you and I thank you.

Kindness is the greatest gift of all, if you can be anything in life, choose to be kind.

All our love and thanks for always Fiona & Gianburrasca xxx

Printed in Great Britain
by Amazon

47831751R00080